P.S.— WE MADE THIS!

super fun crafts that grow
SMARTER + HAPPIER kids!

ERICA DOMESEK

ILLUSTRATED BY STEPH STILWELL

ABRAMS, NEW YORK

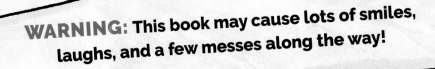

WARNING: This book may cause lots of smiles, laughs, and a few messes along the way!

Editor: Shawna Mullen
Designer: Danielle Youngsmith
Managing Editor: Mike Richards
Production Manager: Larry Pekarek

Library of Congress Control Number: 2022933502

ISBN: 978-1-4197-5610-8
eISBN: 978-1-64700-863-5

Printed and bound in China
10 9 8 7 6 5 4 3 2 1

Abrams books are available at special discounts when purchased in quantity
for premiums and promotions as well as fundraising or educational use.
Special editions can also be created to specification. For details, contact
specialsales@abramsbooks.com or the address below.

Abrams® is a registered trademark of Harry N. Abrams, Inc.

ABRAMS The Art of Books
195 Broadway, New York, NY 10007
abramsbooks.com

FOR WYLIE

P.S.- **You made me a mama!**

Here's to a lifetime of making memories, colorful art projects, fun recipes, with so much love and giggles along the way.

CONTENTS

INTRODUCTION

There are two types of people in the world: people who craft and people who don't craft but want to craft as a way to spend time and connect with their kids. **Here's the good news: This book is for *everyone*.** You don't need to be artistic or imaginative to navigate these projects and recipes—and if you are, well, you get a pat on the back. It's also worth noting that *zero* of these projects contain glitter. (You're welcome.)

This book is a colorful resource for anyone who needs an engaging activity to do with kids any day of the week. It's meant to inspire, to encourage play, and to nurture creativity. There are so many life lessons that can be learned by using your hands, upcycling, sparking imagination, and repurposing existing items in the home. At the end of the day, making things shouldn't be hard—it should be fun. Consider this your invitation to roll up your sleeves, to let things get messy, and to connect with your kids. It doesn't have to be elaborate or expensive.

We're all living in a fast-paced, screen-centered world. So we think it is more important than ever to remember the value of using your hands to create something. As adults and parents, we're increasingly protective of who and what gets our attention, and why. The same framework applies to our children. Raising my three-year-old son, I often ask myself, "What will Wylie get from this? How will it help him learn? How will he grow?" To help me unpack this further in the context of this crafty book, I enlisted Dr. Laurel Felt, resident PhD and senior fellow at the UCLA Center for Scholars and Storytellers. She's an expert in children's media, play, and learning, not to mention a hardworking mom. Dr. Felt and I share the same sensibility about how **arts and crafts is a vehicle for so much more than just hanging drawings on the refrigerator.** You will see that each project has takeaways that are clearly labeled. Let them be gentle reminders that it's not always *what* you're doing or creating, it's about how we can learn from the experience.

It's easy to fall into the social media trap where it seems that every project we do with our kids must be a perfectly executed Pinterest moment. **Whether you're encouraging solitary play on a rainy day or hosting an afternoon playdate for kids in the neighborhood, there's something in these pages for everyone.** The activities and recipes on these pages will jumpstart sensory exploration, pretend play, and STEAM activities (Science, Technology, Engineering, Art, and Math)—all while yielding big smiles and meaningful outcomes. Yes, everything is focused on fun in the book, but it's also designed to help kids become better humans.

The other day my son was crying hysterically, "I just want a cupcake!" We had no cupcakes in our house. I tried calming him down and said, "Let's see if we can make one." We took a mini blueberry muffin, put a tiny dollop of Nutella on top and added sprinkles, and voilà! A cupcake. What does this prove? Raising tiny humans is an emotional rollercoaster, sure, but the littlest dash of creativity and using whatever is already living inside your cabinets can really go a long way, no matter what may be happening under your roof.

Shop your closets, open your pantry, dip into your recycling bin, repurpose that old T-shirt, save that cardboard box, and simply breathe creative new life into items that are sitting idly in your home. Treat this book as you would a beloved cookbook or travel guide. Refer to it often. Dog-ear your favorite pages and take notes. Gift it to someone in your life who could use some extra fun. All you need is an open mind. Don't overthink it. Art is a beautiful thing. At the end of the day, **we're all kids at heart who need an artistic outlet,** and a reason to spend quality time together so we can say, *P.S.-* **We Made This!**

—ERICA DOMESEK

DEVELOPMENTAL TAKEAWAYS
FOR GROWING SMARTER + HAPPIER KIDS

DR. LAUREL FELT, PhD
Childhood Play & Learning Expert

Art experiences provide opportunities to stretch, discover, and grow! **We went through and tagged each project with "takeaways,"** so you can understand all the incredible associated benefits. And yes, **arts + crafts has tons of benefits** other than smiles! Get excited.

We believe that focusing on what your kids are making is as important as why they are making it. It may suprise you to learn that this book was created for adults as much as it was for kids. Yes! Adults sometimes need small reminders that little milestones and tiny educational moments can be incorporated into everyday life for our children and for us! And the best part is, **you do not have to be artistic to get involved.** Phew!

Arts and crafts are fun, but, while they are creating and building, your **kids will also learn skills that will help them in daily life.** For example, take the super cute piggy banks on page 56. Let's focus on how making the

piggy bank offers you and your child a chance to learn about and discuss:

* Favorite animals (IDENTITY)
* Animals' key features (BIOLOGY)
* Money and saving (FINANCIAL LITERACY)
* Shapes and counting (MATH)
* Color and style (ART)
* Words and letters (LITERACY)
* Re-use and upcycling (ENVIRONMENTAL STEWARDSHIP)
* Your first piggy bank (IDENTITY)

Completing a project together supports bonding. The steps alone nurture independence. And admiring the finished product not only boosts kids' pride, it reinforces big ideas like, "We have fun together" and "I can do great things."

We have done all the heavy lifting for you, combining Erica's unparalleled and creative ideas with my master's degree in child development and my PhD in twenty-first-century learning. We believe that anyone who has kids, loves kids, or is a kid should get involved with this book. **Use the Takeaways as a resource all the time,** and most importantly, never stop creating.

CRACK THE CODE!

Look for these Takeaway icons at the top of every project. We'll discuss each one in more detail on the following pages.

COGNITIVE SKILLS

 APPRECIATION FOR NATURE

 ENVIRONMENTAL STEWARDSHIP

 SCIENCE

 MATH

 SPATIAL RECOGNITION

 LITERACY

PHYSICAL SKILLS

 NUTRITION AND NOURISHMENT

 FITNESS

 HEALTH

 THE SENSES

SOCIAL-EMOTIONAL SKILLS

 IDENTITY

 IMAGINATIVE AND CREATIVE PLAY

 CHARACTER STRENGTHS AND LIFE SKILLS

 THE ARTS

 COMMUNITY AND SOCIAL STUDIES

CALLOUTS

 THROWBACK

 QUICKIE PROJECT

 NEEDS ADULT SUPERVISION

COGNITIVE SKILLS

APPRECIATION FOR NATURE

Appreciating nature—animals, plants, weather, and more—offers all sorts of potential benefits: piquing kids' interest in screen-free experiences, developing their scientific habits of mind, supporting their caregiving skills, exercising their bodies, restoring calm (forest bathing is real!).

Animals, plants, weather

ENVIRONMENTAL STEWARDSHIP

Environmental stewardship combines multiple capacities, including appreciating nature, honoring community, and engineering. Hands-on experiences with sustainability from a young age can help it become a more widely embraced value and lifestyle.

Upcycling, recycling, living sustainably

SCIENCE

"Science play" can cultivate curiosity, critical-thinking skills, and subject-matter expertise. It also supports kids' "science identity"—their ability to see themselves as science learners who know and understand science, can use scientific tools and "do" science, and are recognized by gatekeepers as belonging in science. Some identify science identity as the driver of achievement and participation in STEM (science, technology, engineering, and math), especially for individuals from underrepresented groups.

Physics, biology, chemistry, engineering, archaeology, astronomy, technology

MATH

Painting a pattern, sorting and classifying materials, counting items, and other forms of "math play" can help children develop powerful skills. Excelling in math predicts later academic achievement, which is related to numerous positive outcomes.

Counting, measurement, logic

SPATIAL RECOGNITION

Playing with dimension, turning something flat (2D) into something that "pops out" (3D), is not only exciting, it's "mathletic"! Mentally rotating shapes and considering an object's footprint in space are important for academic subjects like geometry and physics, as well as STEM (science, technology, engineering, and math) careers like engineering and architecture. This type of play also cultivates perspective-taking (literally, seeing from an alternate point of view), which can help kids to understand others and exercise empathy.

Shapes, transformation

LITERACY

Literacy activities, which might look like storytelling, book making, alphabet exploration, and more, can boost kids' interest in, attitudes toward, and achievement around reading and writing. Since reading and writing are central to survival in the twenty-first century, that's nothing to sneeze at.

Storytelling, reading, writing

SOCIAL-EMOTIONAL SKILLS

IDENTITY

Cultivating a strong sense of identity, or knowing and liking oneself, can protect kids from engaging in risky or self-destructive behaviors and help them to form healthy relationships.

Understanding family, sense of self, self-esteem

CHARACTER STRENGTHS AND LIFE SKILLS

Practicing social-emotional learning (SEL) skills, which include (but are not limited to) self-awareness, self-management, social awareness, relationship skills, and responsible decision-making, helps kids to understand and care for themselves as well as "play nice with others." Lifelong success, however you define it, starts with SEL.

Self-awareness, empathy, teamwork, curiosity

COMMUNITY AND SOCIAL STUDIES

Honoring community—which encompasses respecting diverse cultures, traditions, and celebrations; understanding different types of paid and unpaid work; and welcoming opportunities to learn and give back—is essential for responsible global citizens. When kids appreciate the profound ways in which we're connected to one another, they are empowered to pursue social justice and peace.

Cultural respect, recognition

IMAGINATIVE AND CREATIVE PLAY

Pretend play gives children the opportunity to flex their creative muscles, create or interpret their own stories (hello, literacy skills!), and practice social and emotional skills as they take on characters' perspectives and/or relate to playmates.

Role play, symbolic play

THE ARTS

Exploring the arts lets kids express their thoughts and feelings, navigate immersive experiences, practice new skills, and appreciate diverse people and cultures.

Music, studio art, design

PHYSICAL SKILLS

FITNESS

HEALTH

NUTRITION AND NOURISHMENT

According to just about everybody's grandmothers (and my belly when I'm hangry), food is everything: culture, love, survival, and more. Learning about food and exploring the art of cooking—even if only for pretend—can bust kids' buttons with pride and enhance their food literacy, or their understanding of the impact of their food choices on their health, the environment, and our economy.

Food, cooking, nutrition

Gross motor skills—abilities that let us move large muscles in our torso, legs, and arms—are incredibly important for healthy development and holistic well-being. Their hallmarks, like physical strength, agility, balance, and coordination, allow our kids to move safely and competently through the world so they can execute vital practical tasks (like unpacking groceries) and enjoy lifelong leisure activities (like sports, dance, and hiking). Because our kids' physical, cognitive, and social-emotional functioning are interconnected, like a chain, one might argue that they're only as strong as their weakest link.

Strength, agility, coordination, sports

Exploring aspects of health, from exercise to disease to mindfulness, can help kids to better manage their own wellness, educate and inspire family members, and feel at home in their bodies.

Nutrition, exercise, mindfulness, hygiene, anatomy

THE SENSES

Sensory play, or play that's about engaging one's sense of touch, taste, sight, sound, and/or smell, is enormously important for meeting some children's needs around sensory stimulation, helping children learn how to process sensory input, and delighting and relaxing others (blissed-out slime squishing, anyone?).

Sight, touch, hearing

CALLOUTS

THROWBACK

No school like the #oldskool! This "oldie but a goodie" project treats nostalgic grownups to all the feels, gives their brains a break (no need to look at the book—you got this!), and rolls out the red carpet for intergenerational storytelling ("When I was little, I did this same project . . .").

QUICKIE PROJECT

Taking 20 minutes or less, a quickie project is the solution to some of #kidlife's trickier questions, like "What should we do with this odd chunk of time?" and "Given my kid's (and my own!) limited attention span, what's a project we can handle?" Kids will love the easy-peasy process and the tangible product; caregivers will love the low-maintenance prep and clean up!

NEEDS ADULT SUPERVISION

While fun is always essential, safety is the utmost importance. Some projects and recipes will require an adult to supervise and/or help with certain materials and tools. Craft knives, sharp scissors, hot glue guns, kitchen appliances, and more are imporant to help execute projects and recipes, but not at the cost of a boo-boo.

ARE YOU READY?
OKAY, GREAT!

- - - - - - - - - - - - - - - - - - - -

☑ Roll up your sleeves . . .

☑ Put those screens down (sorry, not sorry!)

☑ You are about to do some amazing projects!

P.S.- **Don't forget:**

﹡ Some projects require help from adults
  (don't worry, they are all labeled for you)

﹡ Safety first (be extra careful with glue guns
  and cutting tools, and in the kitchen)

﹡ Non-toxic glues, paints, markers, and
  materials are always the way to go

﹡ Living a more sustainable life by up-cycling
  household items and reinventing them helps
  our planet

﹡ Make sure to take pics of your amazing
  creations + share with @psimadethis

﹡ Most important . . . HAVE FUN!

THE PROJECTS

DID SOMEONE SAY SPECIAL DELIVERY?

Raise your hand if you have a bevy of boxes that get delivered to your home daily. Instead of tossing them, save your boxes for future creations that require just some artsy imagination and a whole lot of smiles! From personalized pizzas to dinos that can dance to ride-along ice cream trucks, boxes know no boundaries. It's all about using your creative juices to upgrade playful projects and transforming plain cardboard into creative wonders. It's easy to think outside the box when you have your crayon, paint, and scissor friends to help you out.

P.S.- **Always remember to recycle. Every project in this chapter is an opportunity to reinvent a material while being sustainable.**

BRICK OVEN PIZZA

Your very own cardboard pizza pie? That's amore!

INGREDIENTS

Cardboard box · cardboard · scissors · construction paper · glue · marker

1. Use a marking tool to trace a semicircle on the side of the box and use scissors to cut it out.

2. Cut out flame shapes using red, orange, and yellow construction paper. Layer and glue the shapes together to create "hot flames."

3. Draw bricks on the outside of the "oven" opening using a marker, and glue the flames to the inside walls of the box.

4. Draw and cut out a pizza paddle using a large piece of cardboard. Make your own pizza base and toppings out of colored paper for amazing custom pizzas!

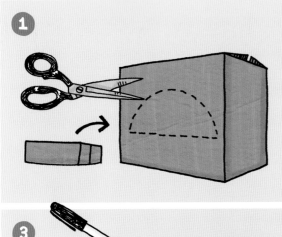

P.S.- Place a smaller box inside the oven to rest the paddle on and to provide a surface for "cooking" the pizza.

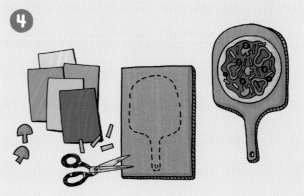

KARAOKE MACHINE + MIC

You'll be the headlining act with your very own karaoke machine.

INGREDIENTS

Cardboard box • paper towel roll tube • scissors • aluminum foil • duct tape • painter's tape • colored paper tape • bottle caps • string • marker • glue

1. Draw a round speaker and a control panel directly onto a box using a marker. Glue beverage caps onto the box for ON/OFF/VOLUME knobs. Get wild! Add stickers, paint, and tape to customize.

2. To make the microphone, decorate a paper towel roll using colorful tape and stickers. Make a ball of aluminum foil and insert it into one end of the tube, securing it with tape. Add details like gems, stickers, and tape for a rockstar finish.

P.S.-
For an extra layer of detail, tape a long string inside the microphone before you break out in song!

ICE CREAM TRUCK + POPSICLES

I scream, you scream . . . we all scream for ice cream!

INGREDIENTS

Wagon • **cardboard** • **scissors** • **paint** • **paintbrush** • **duct tape** • **marker**

1. Draw and cut a panel for the ice cream truck base out of a large piece of cardboard (big enough to hide the wagon). Paint the ice cream truck with fun bright colors! Create the window by cutting the top and sides of the window and folding the flap to the back. Cut some slots to hold "ice cream treats" as shown.

2. Draw and cut out a decorative awning slightly longer than the window width out of a piece of cardboard. Tape or glue the awning above the window. Draw and cut out popsicles and ice creams from spare cardboard. Decorate them using paint, scrap paper, or markers and tape to real popsicle sticks!

3. After everything is dry, use duct tape to secure the cardboard truck panel to one side of the wagon. If you don't

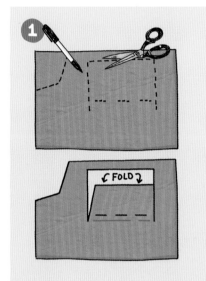

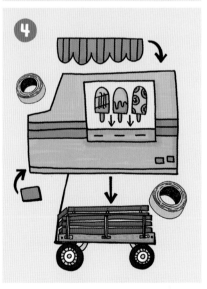

want to use tape, and your wagon has slat openings, poke holes into the cardboard panel and tie it on with string.

4. Place the ice creams into pre-cut slots on the window flap.

DINO SCULPTURES

Rawr! Bring your very own prehistoric pals to life.

INGREDIENTS

Cardboard • scissors • construction paper • crayons • markers • glue

1. Draw and cut out lovable dino (or animal) bodies with heads and, separately, arch-shaped legs. Cut 2 small slits on the bottoms of each dino body and one small slit in the tops of each pair of legs, equal in length.

2. Use leftover cardboard scraps, construction paper, crayons, and markers to decorate the dino pals. Connect the bodies by lining up the leg and body slits, and make your dino come to life!

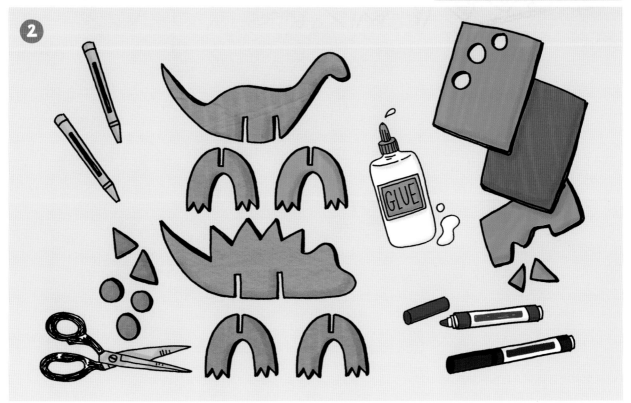

STUFFED ANIMAL SAILBOAT

Ahoy! Set sail with a few furry friends.

INGREDIENTS

Cardboard boxes • wrapping paper or fabric roll tube • fabric • paper cup • straws • scissors • tape • hot glue • felt • rice • pencil

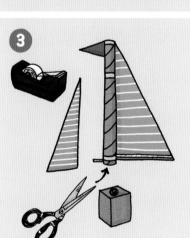

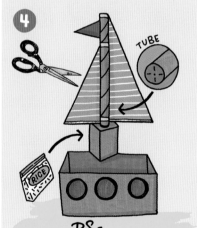

1. Remove the cardboard flaps at the top of the box. Using a cup, trace holes for portholes and cut them out.

2. Trace and cut out two tall fabric triangles (one taller than the other) and fold them in half vertically. Glue together the outside edges of the tallest triangle and attach a straw to the bottom edge for sail stability. Repeat for the second sail.

3. Tape each sail to the paper tube, which will be the boat's mast. Make a tiny hole near the bottom of the tube so you can insert the straws to help with stability. (Trim the straws down to fit.)

4. Cut a hole the size of the tube in the top of a small box and secure the tube in the

hole.✳ You may need to add a few pieces of tape around the tube and box to help stabilize them. Place the mast (small box and paper tube together) inside the bottom of the boat (the larger box) to set sail!

P.S.-
You can fill the little box with something heavy (like a baggie of rice) or glue the mast to the bottom of the box if you want to keep it more stable. Fill with your favorite stuffed animal passengers and set sail!

✳ Be sure to not cut the opening too large—you want the tube to fit tight.

BUTTERFLY FAIRY WINGS

Take flight in the great outdoors with your very own butterfly wings.

INGREDIENTS

Cardboard • **marker** • **craft knife** • **colored cellophane or tissue paper** • **paint** • **paintbrush** • **scissors** • **ribbon or string**

1. Draw a magical butterfly outline on a flat piece of cardboard and cut out. Be sure to leave space between both wings for the butterfly straps.

2. Paint the butterfly. After it is dry, draw and cut out shapes in the wings, leaving space between each section so the cardboard doesn't rip. Try to have the cutouts mirror each other on both sides, if possible.✳

3. Now for the magic! Cut out cellophane pieces slightly larger than each opening and glue them on the back side of the wings. You should have about ½ inch extra around the outside for the glue.

4. Poke 2 pairs of holes at the center of the wings. Thread string or ribbon through the holes to create straps and knot to secure (think backpack!). Take your wings outside and fly through the sunlight like the beautiful butterfly you are!

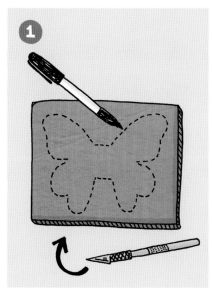

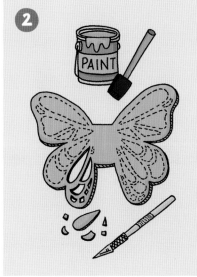

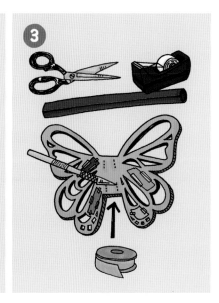

✳ Hey kiddos! Tell your adults that they are the ones who are in charge of using the craft knife!

MAGIC CASTLE

No need for fairy tales, this is a DIY royal treatment we all deserve to dive into!

INGREDIENTS

Cardboard box • paper towel roll tubes • hot glue gun • scissors • paint • paintbrush • craft knife • stickers • rhinestones • string

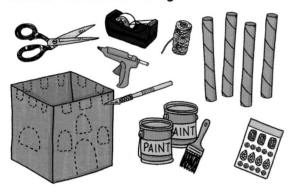

1. Remove the cardboard flaps at the top of the box. Cut out squares along the top of the box to create the castle wall. Cut out full windows and a door wherever you'd like.

2. Paint the castle and its separate pillars (the paper towel rolls). When dry, cut slits at the bottom of the pillars so they can be placed on each corner of the castle. Add details to the towers with glued-on pieces of colored construction paper.

3. Add royal finishes such as stickers and rhinestones. Then go wild and add a drawbridge with string!

P.S.- For the door, cut all but the bottom edge to create a drawbridge.

POP-UP SHOP

Whether it's a bakery, a lemonade stand, or a sandwich shop—you're the boss!

INGREDIENTS

Cardboard box • craft knife • egg carton • tissue box • construction paper • paint • paintbrush • scissors • toilet paper roll tube • bottle caps • hot glue gun • colored paper tape • marker • pencil

1. Cut out flaps on one side of the tall box that will turn into a "pick-up window."

2. Paint the outside. Add a store name and fun designs.

3. After the paint is dry, tape out separate sections that allow everyone to "Read the menu," "Place your order," "Pick up," and "Pay up!" Get creative with imaginary play and create menus on separate pieces of paper and cut additional slots for money.

P.S.-
Have some fun after your new appliance or furniture arrives and reimagine it into your dream shop! The bigger the box, the bigger the shop.

BIG BOX ALERT!

P.S.-
Egg cartons are the new keypads.

CHALKBOARD LAPTOP

Less screen time, more time for creativity at your fingertips.

INGREDIENTS

Cardboard • scissors • chalk paint • paintbrush • painter's tape • ruler • glue • marker • chalk

1. Cut out a long rectangle of cardboard and fold it in half crosswise for the laptop body, or use two connected sides of an existing box. Draw an outline for the screen (top), keyboard (bottom), and track pad (bottom)

2. Tape a 1-inch (2.5-cm) border around the top "screen" and "track pad" and paint the inside of each with chalkboard paint. Cut out smaller squares for keyboard keys. Glue them down and let dry completely.

3. Once the chalk paint is completely dry it's time to draw on the screen with chalk and play. It's a great way to work on alphabet skills, numbers, and even office memos!

P.S.- They don't have to be perfect or 100 percent accurate. A space bar and some buttons will do the trick!

FOLD

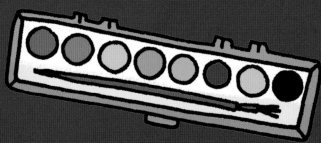

E-Z EASELS

Channel your inner Picasso and paint whatever strikes your fancy (pizza not included).

INGREDIENTS

Pizza box • extra cardboard—same size as pizza box lid • craft knife • painter's tape • duct tape • chip clips • paper • paint • paintbrush • water

1. Tape up all edges of the extra piece of cardboard with painter's tape

2. Make a triangle as shown below by duct-taping the extra cardboard to the two sides of the open pizza box.

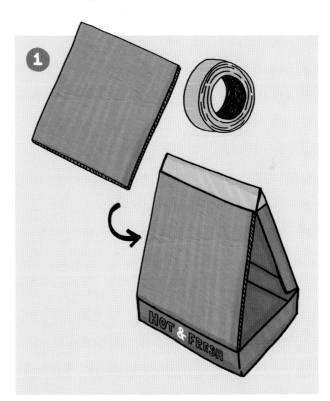

P.S.-
Attach one or two chip clips at the top to help secure a bunch of paper (see option 1)—or, tape down individual sheets with painter's tape. You can sit the easel on its side (see option 2) and tape paper on all three sides for a triple-threat creative project, too! Kick it up a notch and attach a pencil holder with coloring tools to allow for creative moments at any time.

OPTION 1 — TWO-SIDED

OPTION 2 — THREE-SIDED

PLINKO BOARD

You don't need to wait for a get-together to get this together—any day can be game day!

INGREDIENTS

Cardboard · wrapping paper tubes · paper cups · ping-pong balls · straws · hot glue gun

1. Lay a long piece of cardboard, about the length of the wrapping paper tubes you are using, on a flat surface and hot-glue wrapping paper tubes to the two long sides to make bumpers.

2. Hot-glue straws at alternating angles down the panel, leading to different drop-off points, with a cup underneath each drop-off point. Prop the board up at an angle to play.

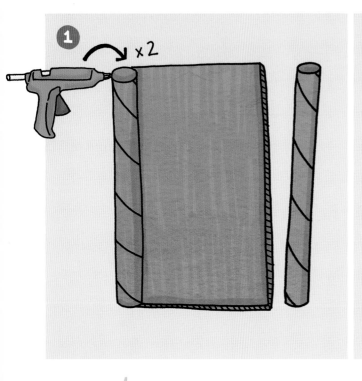

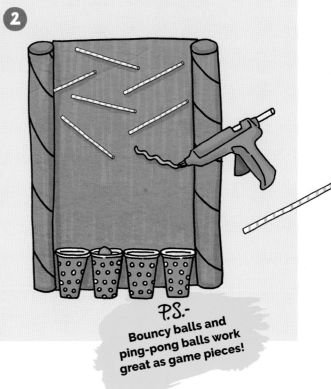

P.S.-
Bouncy balls and ping-pong balls work great as game pieces!

COOL BUS

The destination is up to you—and your imagination!

INGREDIENTS

Cardboard boxes • cardboard • construction paper • black tape • disposable pie pan • paper plates • paint • paintbrush • hot glue gun • scissors

1. Grab three cardboard boxes—extra-large, for the body of the bus, large, for the front of the bus, and medium, for the stop sign. Trace and cut out side windows and the front window from the extra-large box using a craft knife or scissors.

2. Paint both the extra-large box and the large box yellow. After they dry, glue the large box to the front of the extra-large box, underneath the front window.

3. Make the stop sign and add construction paper and cardboard details to the bus as shown. Attach using hot glue, then decorate with markers. Get creative with things that you may have at home such as paper plates, disposable pie pans, and foil!

P.S.- Save the medium box for making stop a sign and save the cardboard scraps for making other details.

YOU DO YOU!

BRUSHING BUDDY STATION

Brushing your teeth and hair is more fun with a buddy.

INGREDIENTS

Cardboard · **clear packing tape** · **scissors** · **hot glue gun** · **hole puncher** · **paint** · **paintbrush** · **beans (dry)** · **string or yarn** · **markers**

1. Draw a face with an open mouth onto a piece of cardboard and cut it out. Paint the face.

2. Once it is dry, cover the entire face with clear packing tape, folding any excess tape around to the back. After the face is finished you can draw special features (freckles, eye shadow, jewelry, etc.) repeatedly using washable markers. Wipe off each time with a moist towel and start fresh.

3. Punch holes around the top curve of the head and knot string or yarn through to create hair. Add teeth by gluing beans directly onto the mouth.

P.S.-
It's fun to cut and style the hair just like your own!

DIRTY LAUNDRY DUNK

Be the MVP of laundry or make laundry chores a slam dunk!

INGREDIENTS

Cardboard • scissors • craft knife • hot glue gun • colored paper tape • pencil • double-sided adhesive or command hooks

1. Draw a backboard shape onto one piece of cardboard and cut out using a craft knife.

2. Use colored tape to make a backboard design.

3. Fold the second piece of cardboard as shown to make the "net." (Optional: Cut a zig-zag bottom.)

4. Glue the net to the backboard. Attach the net and backboard above the hamper using double-sided adhesive, duct tape, or command hooks and string.

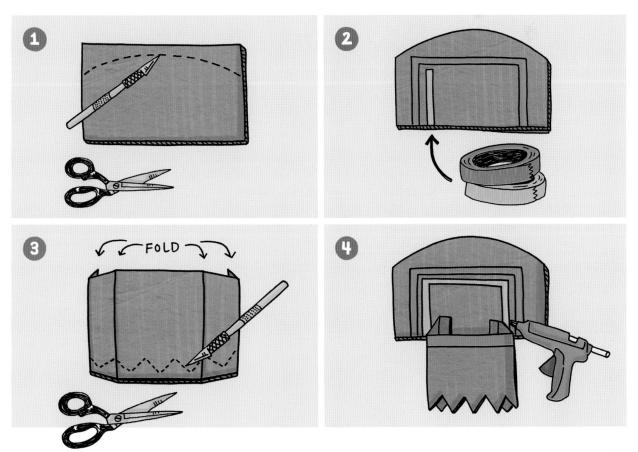

FOLD

WHEN THE CEREAL IS DONE, IT'S TIME TO START THE FUN!

From cereal boxes to egg cartons and detergent containers to toilet paper rolls, these are a few of the crafty ingredients that already live inside your home and are just waiting to be reinvented. There's no better time to turn those wooden spoons into puppets and use shower squeegees as an epic paint tool—nothing is off-limits at this house party! Okay, well, maybe Mom's lipstick . . .

BINOCULARS + SCAVENGER HUNT

**Create, explore, and conquer! Indoors or outdoors, anything goes.
Bonus points if your clues include all five senses.**

INGREDIENTS

Toilet paper roll tubes · construction paper · scissors · colored paper tape · hole puncher · string · stapler · markers · stickers · pencil · glue

1. Decorate two toilet paper rolls with colored paper using glue, adding decorative tape and stickers.

2. Staple the rolls together (from the inside) to make a sturdy pair of binoculars.

3. Punch two holes in the outside edges of your binoculars. Thread a piece of string through the holes and knot on the inside.

4. Create an epic scavenger hunt: Make a list of items to find (indoors or outdoors) on a fun hunt with friends!

PARROT PETS

Polly want a crafter?! **These pets are sure to inspire hours of creative play.**

INGREDIENTS

Toilet paper roll tubes • construction paper • pipe cleaners • scissors • craft knife • hole puncher • feathers • glue • tape • marker • pencil

1. Wrap and glue or tape two-thirds of a toilet paper roll with one color of construction paper and glue a contrasting color to the remaining third.

2. Cut out an oval with a flat bottom for the chest, circle for eyes, and a triangle for the beak and glue or tape on. Googly eyes will also work!

3. Glue or tape feathers to each side for wings and one on the inside for the crest on top of the bird's head.

4. Punch two small holes in the bottom of the bird and thread pipe cleaners through so you can attach the parrot to your wrist or a branch and make it your puppet pal. Don't forget to add little legs out of pipe cleaners, too!

SELF-PORTRAIT X-RAY

Recycle old paper towel rolls and put your creative bones to work:
Proof that old paper towel rolls are good down to the bone.

INGREDIENTS

Paper roll • paper towel roll tubes • toilet paper roll tubes • scissors • hot glue gun • construction paper • glue • yarn • marker • pencil

1. Unfurl a large piece of paper from your paper roll and tape it to the floor or a flat surface.

2. Use toilet paper rolls and paper towel rolls cut into segments to create skeleton joints, fingers, and toes.

3. Tape or glue rolls and segments to the paper in a skeleton shape, starting with the spine. (Sketch it out with a pencil first if you want.) Add a big construction paper heart to the chest and draw your face on the head to prove there is DIY in your DNA!

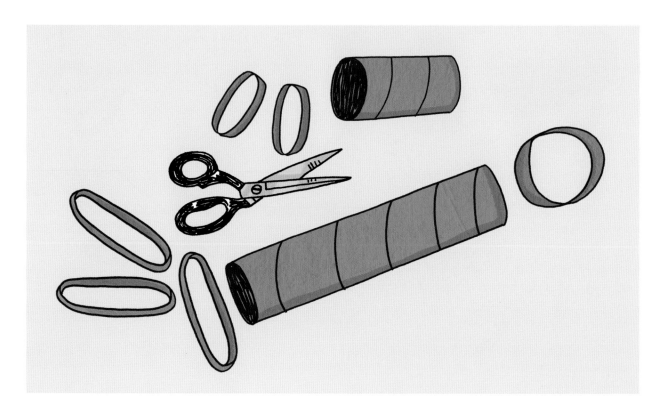

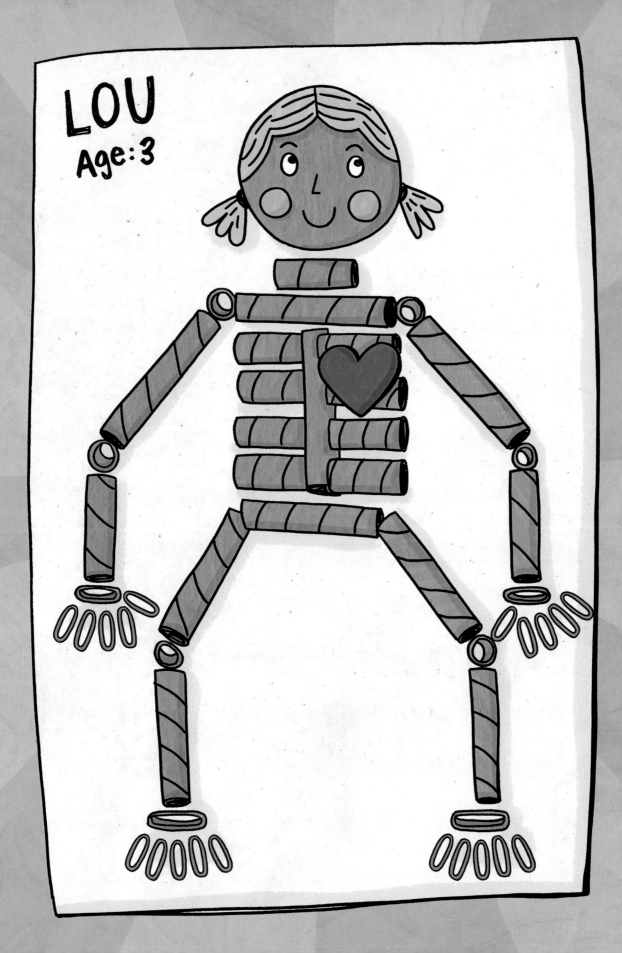

SQUEEGEE ARTWORK

**Shower the walls with unique and colorful creations—
if you can dream it, you can squeegee it.**

INGREDIENTS

Canvas • paint • squeegee

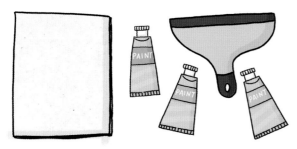

1. Cover the top third of a canvas or plain sheet of paper with paint dots, swirls, and squiggles.

2. While the paint is still wet, pull the squeegee over the paint, from the very top to the bottom, to create a masterpiece! Squeegee again until you have covered the canvas completely.

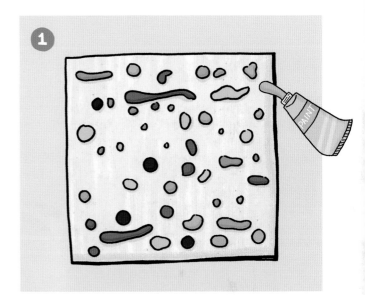

P.S.-
Be careful not to squeegee *too* much, as it may smear the design.

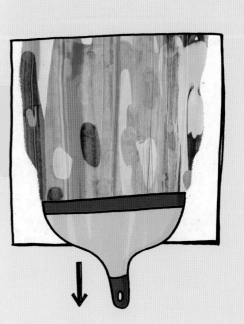

PERSONAL PIGGY BANKS

Stash your hard-earned ca$h inside a fun little friend. You know what they say: *"Moo money, moo problems."*

INGREDIENTS

Oatmeal or bread crumb cylinder • construction paper • aluminum foil • egg carton • scissors • craft knife • paint • paintbrush • hot glue gun • cotton balls • stickers • pipe cleaners • markers

1. Clean the inside of a classic oatmeal or bread crumb cylinder.

2. Dream up your favorite furry animal, or anything that makes you happy, and then decorate the outside of the cylinder with paint, colored paper, and glue to create your design and turn it into a wildly cool bank.

3. Cut a slit in the lid so you can slip in all that cash!

BALLOON ROCKETS

3, 2, 1 . . . get ready for takeoff!

INGREDIENTS

Balloons · construction paper · scissors · straws · tape · pencil

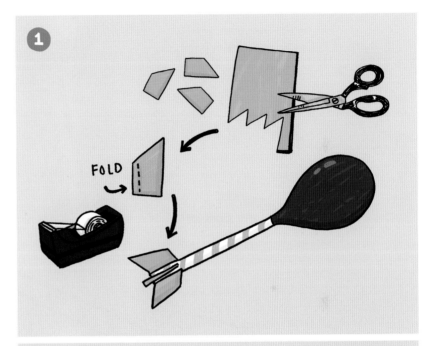

1. Cut 3 small "wings" out of scrap paper. Fold their edges over ½ inch (12 mm) and tape them evenly spaced around the bottom of the straw.

2. Insert the straw into the balloon. Blow air into the straw, filling the balloon. Pinch the bottom of the balloon until you're ready to release.

3. Let it soar into the air and see whose balloon can fly farther!

STRAW ART

Straight from the juice box to the art gallery—anything is possible with a little paint.

INGREDIENTS

Paper, markers • straws • watercolor paint • paintbrush • water • googly eyes • glue

1. Place a sheet of paper for your artwork on a flat surface. Dip a paintbrush into water to saturate, then place the brush directly into watercolor paint. Add a paint blob to the paper.

2. Scatter the paint by blowing into a straw positioned over—but not touching—the paint blob. Keep about 3 inches (7.5 cm) between the straw and paint blob. The air you blow through the straw will move the paint around the page, creating fun shapes. Repeat with more paint blobs.

3. After the paint dries, add a few details to turn your art into a painting of a scary monster, a butterfly, sunshine, a tree— anything goes! Draw on eyes with markers or add googly eyes to really make your cool creatures and animals come to life!

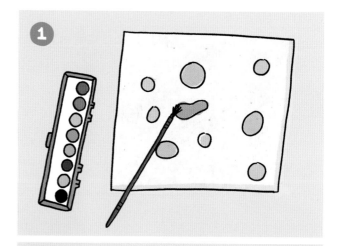

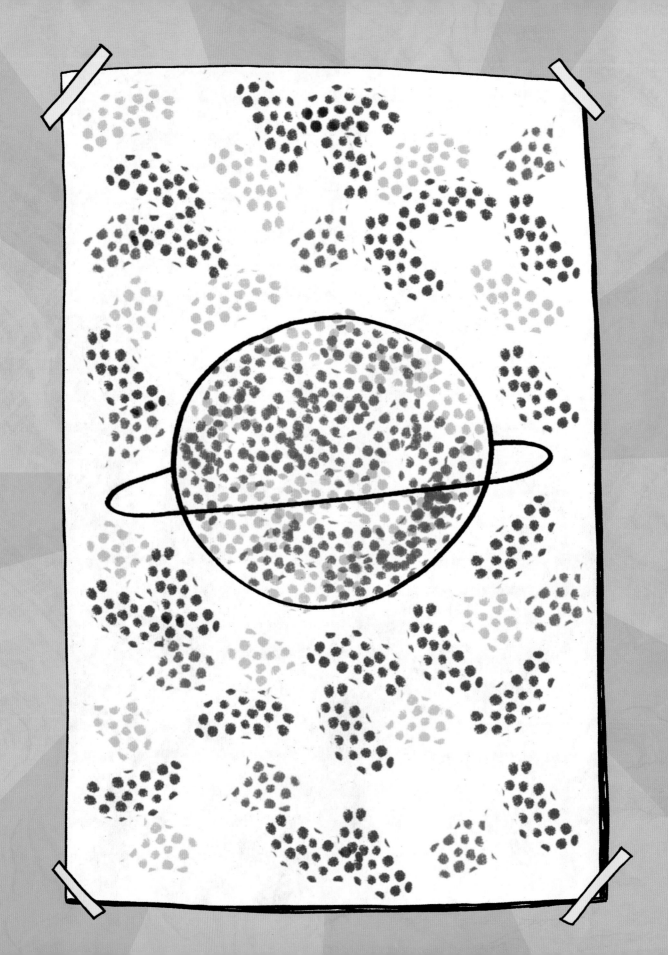

BUBBLE SHOE PAINTING

Paint the town any color you'd like with these bubble wrap "shoes."

INGREDIENTS

Bubble wrap • craft paper • paper plates • painter's tape • paint • pencil

1. Wrap pieces of bubble wrap securely around your feet up to your ankles, covering your feet completely and taping securely around your ankles (do not tape to skin!).

2. Unroll craft paper onto the floor (a large canvas works too!). You can go free-form with color, or use a pencil to trace the outline of an image and then fill it in. Have different colors of paint ready on paper plates: Dip your wrapped feet into the paints, then step on the paper to create artwork. Paint the town red! Or blue, yellow, pink . . .

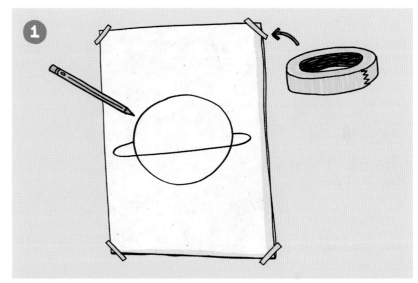

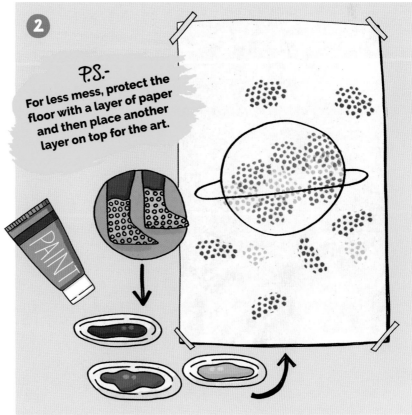

P.S.-
For less mess, protect the floor with a layer of paper and then place another layer on top for the art.

PUPPET PALS

It's a zoo out there . . . stay crafty, kids!

INGREDIENTS

Paper plates • **construction paper** • **scissors** • **hole puncher** • **hot glue gun** • **paints** • **paintbrush** • **markers** • **yarn** • **glue** • **popsicle sticks** • **googly eyes** • **stickers**

1. Grab all the essentials in your toolbox to decorate these cute fans. Making the most of everyday items (googly eyes, construction paper, feathers, string, stickers, markers, paint, yarn, felt, foam paper) is the name of the game. Transform basic paper plates into anything your heart desires, from a playful puppy to a lion cub. Use your imagination!

2. When you are finished, glue a popsicle stick to the back and let dry completely.

TABLE TENNIS

Serve up some fun with personalized paddles.

INGREDIENTS

Table • paper plates • ruler • wooden spoon • painter's tape • tape • balloon • markers • stickers

1. Use markers and stickers to decorate sturdy paper plates with your home team name and chosen symbols. Make one for every player.

2. Tape a ruler or wooden spoon to the back of the plates to create handles.

3. Use low-stick tape to make a centerline on your kitchen—or other—table. Blow up a balloon and use the paddles to hit the balloon back and forth over the tape line.

MAGICAL MICROSCOPE

See things in a new way by repurposing a detergent bottle.

INGREDIENTS

Laundry detergent bottle • paper towel roll tube • cardboard • scissors • craft knife • hot glue gun • tape • marker

1. Grab a large, empty laundry detergent bottle. Draw and cut out a square on the side opposite the handle of the bottle.

2. Cut off the top of the detergent lid and place a paper towel roll through the hole. Secure the roll to the lid with glue.

3. Tape or glue a cardboard square to the bottom of the cutout to be a viewing tray. Collect special items like flowers and shells to view through your new microscope.

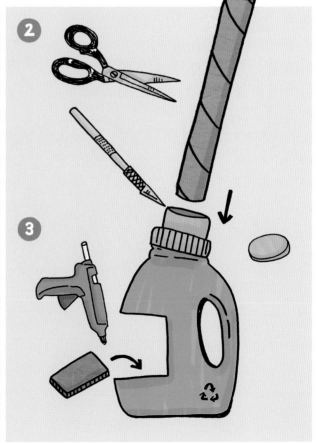

MINI PUPPET THEATER + PUPPETS

Lights, camera, action! Be the star of your own very own theatrical production (after you finish your cereal).

INGREDIENTS

Cereal box • wooden spoons • construction paper • fabric • ribbon • scissors • craft knife • hot glue gun • glue • measuring tape • ruler • paint • paintbrush • pom-poms • googly eyes • paint markers or markers • duct tape

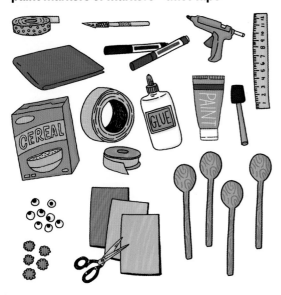

1. Paint a cereal box a fun color, and let the paint dry completely.

2. Draw a rectangle on the front of the box and cut it out. Be sure to leave a 1-inch (2.5-cm) border on the sides and bottom, and a little extra room at the top for the "marquee."

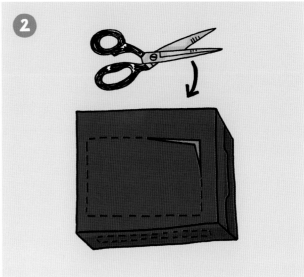

3. Cut a long slit in the bottom of the box for the performers (spoon puppets) to slide into. To make spoon puppets: Paint a wooden spoon a solid color and let it dry completely. Once its dry you can use a paint marker to add details. Glue on googly eyes and fun embellishments like pom-poms and pipe cleaners.

4. For curtains, cut two small pieces of fabric taller than the window and tie a bit of ribbon around the center of each piece. Tape the fabric to the inside of the box and arrange the drapes to make the theater come to life.

MAX'S THEATER

P.S.-
Personalize your theater by decorating a marquee with your name in lights (or marker!)

AIN'T NO PARTY LIKE A GLUE GUN PARTY!

ANIMAL ART MUSEUM

An egg'cellent project with no admission required.

INGREDIENTS

Cardboard · construction paper · egg carton · scissors · craft knife · hot glue gun · glue · paint · paintbrush · colored paper tape · markers · pipe cleaners · cotton balls

1. Cut a frame out of cardboard. Use tape to attach a piece of paper to one side of the frame, this will be the backdrop for your animal. Decorate the front of the frame with colored paper tape or markers.

2. Cut off the bottom egg "bumps" from an empty cardboard egg carton and use them as the base for each animal's head and face. Some animals may require a larger portion of the carton: For example, an elephant with ears may need three "bumps."

3. Once the bumps are cut out, paint and decorate them with faces and ears—even fur. You may need to glue a few pieces together, depending on the exact animal you are making. Look up reference photos online to help you design each animal. Get creative and add cotton balls for bunny faces, pipe cleaners for jellyfish tentacles—look around the house for items that inspire you. When they are finished, attach the animals to the cardboard plaques and frames for an incredible gallery wall.

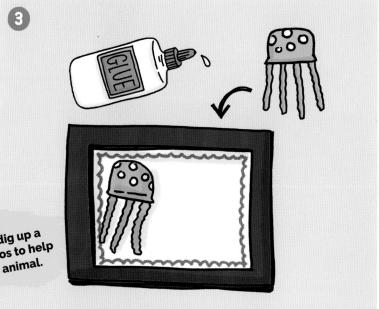

P.S.-
You may need to dig up a few reference photos to help you design each animal.

BUBBLE VASE

Every little's garden starts with a seed (and an egg carton).

INGREDIENTS

Jar • egg carton • scissors • craft knife • hot glue gun • paint • paintbrush

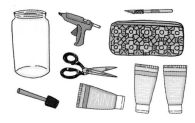

1. Slowly bend a cardboard egg carton around a glass jar; mark and cut the carton to fit around the jar with about a 1-inch (2.5-cm) overlap.

2. Once the carton is cut to the correct size, paint the outside of the egg cups one, two, or as many colors as you like. Let dry completely before bending the carton around the jar and gluing the ends together to make a modern art bubble vase.

3. Add some water and cut flowers—or add potting soil and a sweet succulent that will happily thrive where it is planted.

SHRINKY CHARM JEWELRY

It's a bead! It's a necklace! Oh, wait . . . it's a leftover food container????

INGREDIENTS

Oven • timer • plastic food container • permanent markers • parchment paper • scissors • craft knife • hole puncher • string or ribbon • beads

1. Leftover plastic food containers are worth saving once the food is gone: Use their magical shrinking power to make fun projects. Doodle anything your heart desires on the plastic using permanent markers. Remember that the piece will get smaller when you bake it, so make sure the drawings are large enough that they can still be seen in their (finished) shrunken size.

2. Preheat the oven to 350°F (175°C). Cut out your designs with scissors and place on a parchment-lined baking sheet. Reminder: If you are making charms for jewelry, punch a hole in the design before baking using a hole-punch. Bake the designs for 2 to 3 minutes, and let cool before playing with them or stringing them on a ribbon with beads for a fun charm necklace.

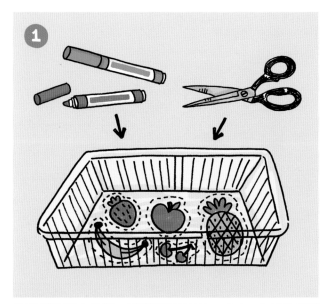

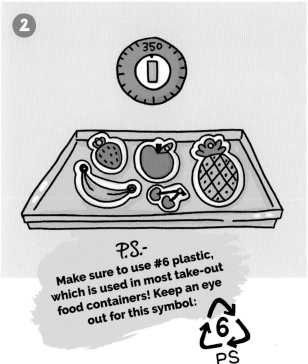

P.S.-
Make sure to use #6 plastic, which is used in most take-out food containers! Keep an eye out for this symbol:

6 PS

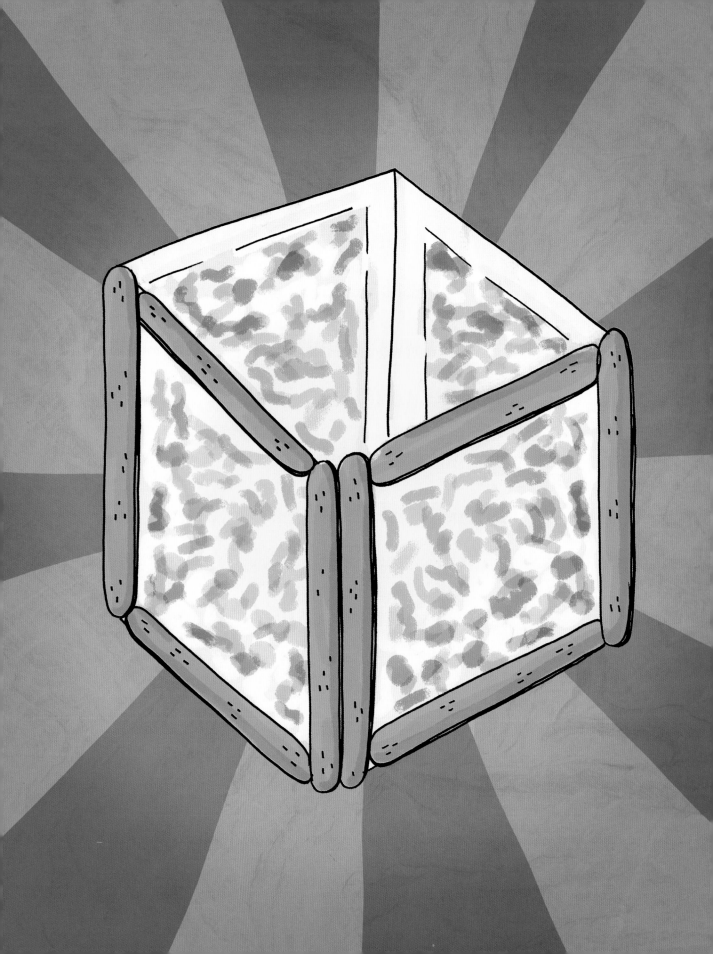

TERRAZZO LIGHT BOX

Popsicle sticks and crayon shavings make for a bright idea.

INGREDIENTS

Printer paper • wax paper • popsicle sticks • iron • scissors • cheese grater (optional) • craft knife • hot glue gun • crayons • pencil • electric tea light

1. Make crayon shavings the old-fashioned way with a cheese grater or, very carefully, with scissors. Sandwich the shavings between two pieces of wax paper and iron the paper "sandwich" on low just until the shavings inside melt together. Place a sheet of plain paper on a hard flat surface, then a layer of wax paper, do the crayon shavings, and then add the top layer of wax paper. Iron on medium heat for a few seconds until the shavings melt. You may need to make a few of these "sandwiches" if they do not all fit on one sheet—you will need five wax squares in all; see Step 2.

2. Let the "sandwich" cool so the wax hardens. Once the wax is hard, glue popsicle sticks directly onto the wax paper, creating five total squares. Cut out each popsicle stick square.

3. Using a hot-glue gun (yes, talking to you, adults!), glue the squares together to make the four sides of a box lantern. Use the last square for the bottom. Place a tea light inside the box to watch your project light up a room.

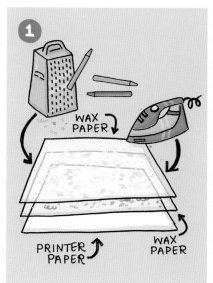

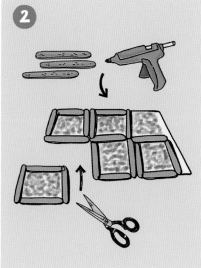

TIE-DYE COFFEE FILTER ART

It's all groovy, baby! Tie-dye with coffee filters to pack in some serious flower power.

INGREDIENTS

Coffee filters • spray bottle • water • pipe cleaners • hot glue gun • stapler • markers

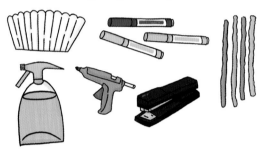

1. Flatten coffee filters and scribble all over them using water-based colored markers. Anything goes!

2. Use a spray bottle filled with water to spritz the decorated filters until the colors bleed together magically. Once the filters are dry, use them for decoration on cards and artwork, or turn them into delicate flowers, flower headbands, or cute caterpillar sun catchers to tape in your windows.

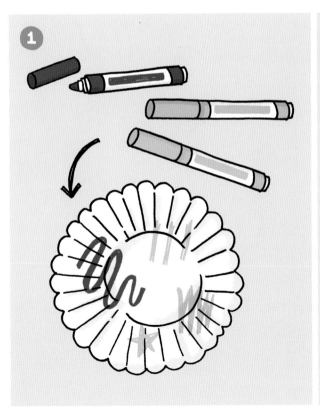

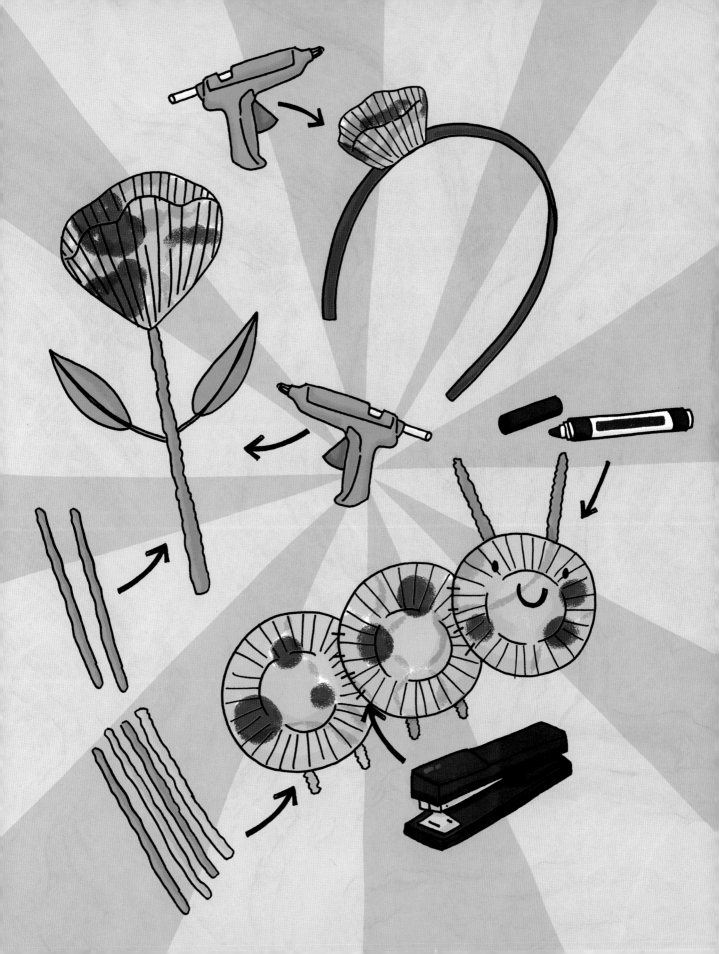

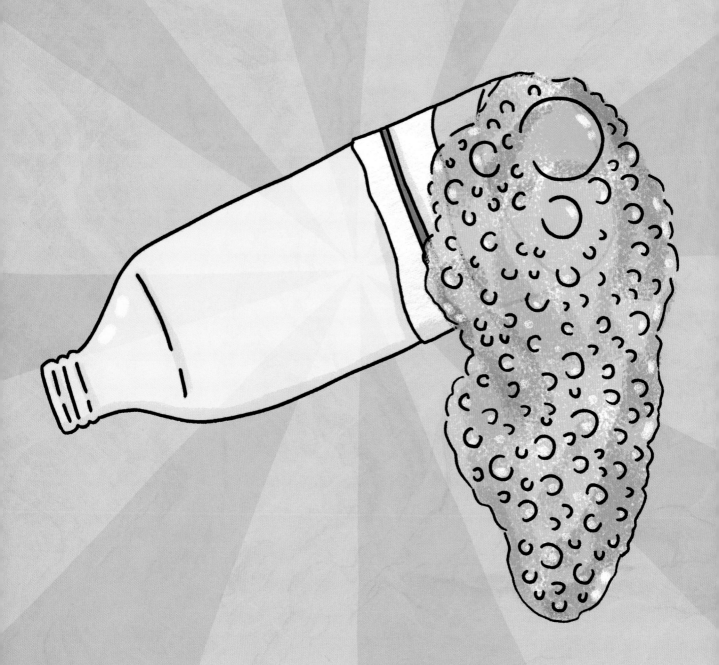

RAINBOW BUBBLE BLOWER

Take to the lawn or to the tub and watch your bubble creations step up their rainbow game.

INGREDIENTS

Plastic water bottle • scissors • craft knife • rubber band • bowl • measuring cup • dish soap • water • whisk • food coloring • sock

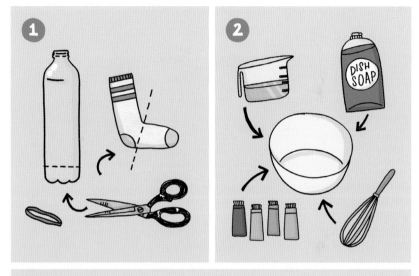

1. Cut off the bottom of a plastic water bottle and affix a sock securely over the opening, using a rubber band.

2. In a shallow bowl or pan, briskly whisk together equal parts water and dish soap to make a bubble solution. Add small dots of food coloring to the mixture and leave them be.

3. Dip the sock-covered end of the water bottle into the bubble solution, and blow through the top of the bottle to witness a delightful burst of colorful bubbles release into the air.

3D PAPER BAG "PETS"

A paper-made pet, while you persuade your parents for the real thing.

INGREDIENTS

**Paper bags · newspaper or tissue paper ·
scissors · stapler · paint · paintbrush · marker**

1. Cut two paper bags along the creases and open each. Lay them flat, on top of one another.

2. Draw the outline of the pet you want to bring to life directly on the top bag, then cut out the shape (keeping both bags together, so that you cut two animals at once). Make sure the shape is the same on the top and bottom bag. Color and decorate your animal—you can do the front-facing side only or the back as well if you're really going for it.

3. After decorating, staple both layers together along the outer edge of the animal, leaving a small opening so you will be able to add stuffing (crumpled newspaper or tissue paper). Stuff the pet, then finish stapling together to seal completely.

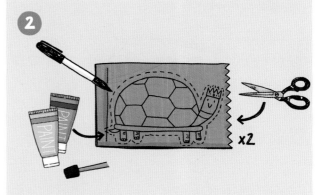

x2

STUFF

RAINBOW CLOUDS + MARBLE SKIES

You'll be floating on cloud nine through these candy-colored DIY skies.

INGREDIENTS

Bowl • shaving cream • water • cups • eye dropper or measuring spoons • food coloring

1. Fill a glass bowl two-thirds with water.

2. Spray shaving cream on top to create fluffy "clouds."

3. Fill smaller cups with water and add one drop of food coloring to each cup and mix.

4. Use an eye dropper or measuring spoon to rain droplets of colored water on or into the shaving-cream cloud and watch the "weather" change from clear blue skies to a chance of rainbow showers.

AND TODAY'S EXPERIMENT IS...

SOAP CLOUDS

Turn an ordinary bar of soap into a mini science project (feel free to wash behind your ears while you're at it).

INGREDIENTS

Microwave · bar soap · microwave-safe plate

1. Place a new bar of soap on a microwave-safe plate or container.

2. Microwave on high for 1 to 2 minutes, and an out-of-this-world cloud will start growing on cue. It's truly wild to watch! Don't forget to take your soap cloud into the tub for a good scrub-a-dub-dub.

OMG! THIS IS SO COOOOOL!

P.S.-
Wait a few minutes to let cool before moving the plate. Contents will be HOT.

THE GREAT
OUTDOORS

FLOWERS, LEAVES, AND ROCKS—OH MY!

Loving Mother Nature is easy when we learn to mindfully respect our planet and its bountiful offerings and beauty. Crafting with found objects from nature is good for the planet, too. Ditch the store-bought plastic in favor of more natural art supplies. Next time you take that nature or beach walk, leave no stone unturned—seriously. Bring home natural gems that can be used for accessible art.

P.S.- **Many of these crafts can be made year-round. You'll notice different things blooming in the spring versus fall, when all the colors start to change.**

MAGIC WANDS

With a stick and pony beads, you'll be casting (good) spells in no time.

INGREDIENTS

Oven • baking tray • aluminum foil • hot glue gun • painter's tape • sticks • pony beads • cookie cutters • paint • paintbrush • stickers

1. Collect sticks! Wipe one clean with a cloth (if dirty or dusty) and paint it in an intricate pattern.

2. While the paint dries, place a star or heart cookie cutter on a foil-lined baking sheet and fill with your favorite colored pony beads.

3. Bake the pony beads according to the package directions, usually 5 to 10 minutes in a preheated 400°F (230°C) oven, but watch closely as baking time may vary.

4. Remove from the oven and let cool completely. Remove the cookie cutter and attach the star or heart to the top of the stick with hot glue. Decorate with stickers, too!

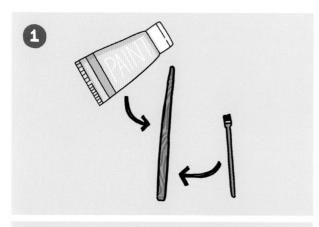

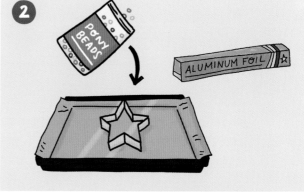

P.S.-
Follow package directions for the pony beads and make sure to have plenty of ventilation while the beads melt. The fumes should not be inhaled.

MEMORY ROCKS GAME

**Making new painted friends and games out of stones you've collected?
That totally rocks!**

INGREDIENTS

**Rocks • dish soap • water • paper towels • hot
glue gun • paint • paintbrush • paint markers •
googly eyes**

1. Wash the rocks (flat ones work best) and dry thoroughly.

2. Reach for paint and paint pens to doodle anything from vegetables to the alphabet to numbers (for counting). For a memory game, be sure to make two of each icon. Get creative—draw random things and create a story! Or even make separate eye, nose, and lip rocks to make puzzle faces!

3. To play the memory game, turn all the rocks over and flip over one at a time to see if you can score a matching pair!

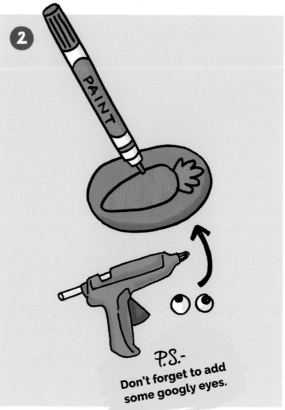

*P.S.—
Don't forget to add
some googly eyes.*

FLOWER PAPER BOWLS

Display flowers from the garden in whole new way that will really bowl people over.

INGREDIENTS

Microwave • flowers • paper towels • plastic wrap • flour • salt • water • scissors • craft knife • balloon • plate • bowl • measuring cup • paint • paintbrush • glue

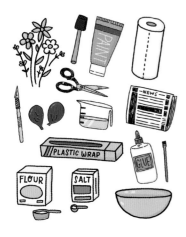

1. Grab a bunch of flowers from the garden. Remove the stems and leaves, then press by sandwiching the flowers between two paper towels and setting a microwave-safe weight on top (like a plate). Microwave in thirty-second intervals (approximately one minute total time) to flatten and dry the flowers.

2. Mix up a batch of papier-mâché (see page 187) and use an inflated balloon as a form to create a bowl shape with the papier-mâché. Leave out to dry fully.

LET DRY

SEAL WITH GLUE

3. When the papier-mâché is dry, pop the balloon and then decorate the inside of the bowl by gluing on the dried flowers. Trim the top edge of the bowl to make the edge smooth.

4. Paint a thin layer of glue all over the now dry bowl to seal the paint. While the glue is still wet, attach dried flowers and let dry: The glue will dry clear.

PRESSED FLOWER LETTER ART

Pressing flowers: It's as easy as A-B-C.

INGREDIENTS

Printer • microwave • flowers • cardboard • plate • paper towels • paper • bowl • glue • paintbrush • marker • frame

1. Collect some flowers and remove the stems and leaves, then press by sandwiching the flowers between two paper towels and setting a microwave-safe weight on top (like a plate). Microwave in thirty-second intervals (approximately one minute total time) to flatten and dry the flowers.

2. Print an extra-large letter, symbol, or a full word on a piece of paper (this will become your flower letter). Attach the paper to the cardboard to create a sturdy backing.

3. Cover the letter, symbol, or word with the dried flowers by using a paintbrush to dab each blossom with a little glue (on the back) and then adhering it to the letter, covering the letter with the flowers entirely. Let dry completely and frame for a flowery personalized artwork.

P.S.- Bold fonts work the best.

CARDBOARD FLOWER VASE

Let your imagination blossom in 3D with fresh flowers and cardboard.

INGREDIENTS

Cardboard • flowers • vines • scissors • craft knife • markers

1. On a piece of cardboard, draw a vase outline and color it using markers.

2. Poke holes at the top for fresh, dried, or faux flowers. You can also add holes along the sides of the vase for greenery.

3. Thread flowers and/or vines through the holes so the flowers look like they are sitting inside and the vines wrap around.

RAINBOW LEAF PRINTS

You won't be able to "leaf" these colorful new friends alone!

INGREDIENTS

Leaves • paper • markers • googly eyes

1. Gather fallen leaves. Using markers, color directly onto the back side of the leaves, covering the surface completely (you are making a stamp).

2. Flip the leaf over so the colored side is down and press it firmly onto a piece of paper, rubbing to transfer the color and design to the paper.

P.S.-
Create fun signs and artwork with googly eyes and stickers!

FLIP & PRESS

USE WHAT YA GOT!

Raise your hand if you're a part of the solo sock club () or the lost glove gang ( ). Before you toss well-worn clothing or accessories, let this be a reminder that you can reinvent things you no longer need to create something you want! Personalizing anything from a T-shirt to a pillowcase is the perfect project for a rainy day, or really any day! Next time you do a closet clean-out or want to jazz up a pair of sneaks, let this be a reminder that breathing new life (and creativity) into items you already own is truly a beautiful thing.

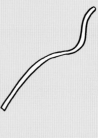

SANDPAPER CRAYON TRANSFERS

Who knew sandpaper and crayons had magical powers!? Create a design and transfer it onto a T-shirt or whatever your heart desires!

INGREDIENTS

Shirt • iron • cardboard • sandpaper • parchment paper • crayons

1. On a piece of lightweight sandpaper, draw a design and color it in with crayons

2. Place the sandpaper crayon-side down on the surface of a cotton T-shirt, cover the sandpaper with a sheet of parchment paper, and iron on low until the crayon transfers to the shirt. Seal the crayon design on the shirt by placing in the dryer at high heat for 30 minutes. Make sure the printed t-shirt is the only item you place in the dryer just in case crayon wax pigment comes off.

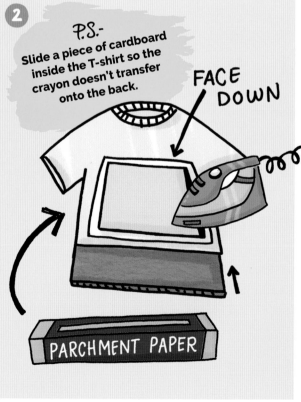

P.S.-
Slide a piece of cardboard inside the T-shirt so the crayon doesn't transfer onto the back.

FACE DOWN

PARCHMENT PAPER

TREE TENT

**An ordinary bedsheet becomes a backyard adventure.
Don't forget your favorite blankets and pillows!**

INGREDIENTS

**Bedsheet • rope • pillows • blankets • large
rocks • duct tape**

1. Wrap one end of a sheet a few feet off the ground around the trunk of a tree and tie it with rope. You may need to use some duct tape to help secure around trunk.

2. Create a tent shape around the base of the tree and hold the sheet in place with rocks.

3. Use the opening where the ends of the sheet meet as a door and anchor with more rocks, so you can easily access the inside the tent.

4. Bring on the cute and cozy vibes with floor pillows and a few blankets.

HAVE FUN WITH IT!

TIE-DYE SHOES + SHOELACES

Give your kicks a groovy new tie-dye vibe.

INGREDIENTS

White canvas shoes • plastic container • gloves • spray bottle • water • rubbing alcohol • eye dropper • markers

1. Draw scribbles and dots onto white shoelaces using permanent markers and spray with a mixture of 1 part water + 1 part rubbing alcohol.

2. Draw shapes, scribbles, lines, and dots with permanent markers on white canvas shoes, leaving some white space to allow the colors to bleed into each other. Spray with the water and rubbing alcohol mixture to encourage the colors to mix and set. Let the shoes dry completely before wearing them.

P.S.- Find a basin, sink, or tub to spray in so mess is minimized.

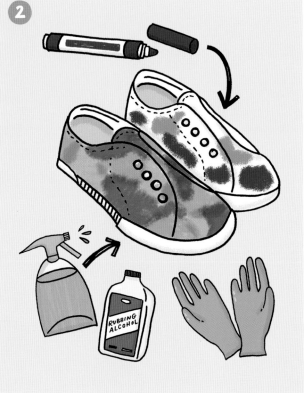

GLOVE MONSTERS

In a few easy steps, a lonely glove becomes a fuzzy new friend.

INGREDIENTS

Glove · **felt** · **scissors** · **hot glue gun** · **tissues** · **markers** · **pom-poms** · **needle and thread** · **googly eyes** · **pencil**

1. Cut off the cuff and then fill the glove with crumpled tissues. Use a pencil to help push the cotton into the fingers of the glove.

2. Fold in each side of the glove's opening and stitch closed.

3. Decorate your monster by gluing on pieces of felt and pom-poms to look like scary eyes, wonky teeth, kooky hair—get wild!

SEW!

DECORATE!

SOCK CATERPILLAR

Transform a sock missing its match!

INGREDIENTS

Sock • felt • scissors • hot glue gun • tissues • rubber bands • pipe cleaners • googly eyes • fabric markers • pencil

1. Stuff a tall solo sock with crumpled tissues to create a round head. Wrap a rubber band around this section so it will hold its shape.

2. Continue to fill sections with tissue and then secure them with a rubber band, filling out the caterpillar segment by segment.

3. Twist a pipe cleaner around the rubber band closest to the "head" and curl the ends for antennas. Glue on googly eyes to let your caterpillar see the world and then decorate with pieces of felt or draw on it directly with fabric markers.

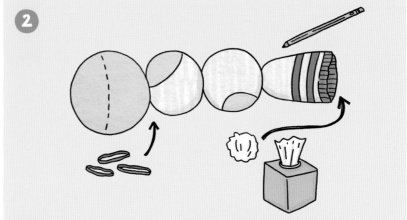

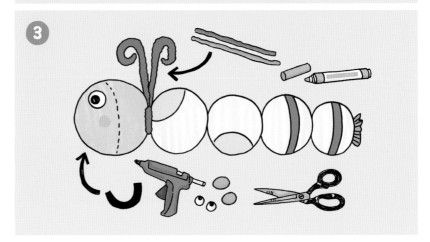

YOU DO HUE!

Paint, crayons, colored paper: A rainbow palette gives ordinary crafts an upgrade, and the best part is, many of these activities don't require a trip to the store. Everything from leftover birthday party balloons to stickers and nearly dry markers are up for grabs and can be used for hours of creative play—then double as bedroom or playroom décor when you're done.

SCRAP-PAPER PICASSOS

Cultivate a little Cubist creativity, piece by piece.

INGREDIENTS

Paper • construction paper • scissors • glue • paint markers • stickers • foam paper shapes • buttons • marker • pencil

1. Trace the outline of a head (any shape goes— there are no rules!) on a piece of paper. Cut funky shapes out of scraps of colored paper and glue the pieces onto the shape to bring an abstract face to life.

2. Layer on stickers, foam paper shapes, and even buttons to bring another dimension to your abstract masterpiece.

COLOR!

ICE CREAM CONE CARDS

A sweet and cool treat that won't melt in the mail.

INGREDIENTS

Paper • paper towels • scissors • watercolor paints • paintbrush • water • markers • pencil

1. Draw hearts!

2. Cut out each heart and fold it in half, down the center, to make a super-sweet ice cream card.

3. Draw delicious cone details, ice cream, and toppings with paint or markers to create your favorite flavors, then write a special message inside.

POOL NOODLE BOATS

Ahoy, matey! With an unused pool noodle, stickers, and markers, you're the captain of your own ship.

INGREDIENTS

Pool noodle • scissors • craft foam • chopstick • colored tape • googly eyes • stickers

1. Cut a pool noodle into two lengths of equal size (approximately 12 inches/30.5 cm each), and tape them side by side with duct tape or paper tape.

2. Cut sails out of craft foam and decorate with stickers, colored tape, and googly eyes!

3. Slice a tiny hole in the top of each sail and insert a chopstick (or a plain stick) through the top and bottom of each sail (leaving about ½ inch/12 mm). Push the stick between the pool noodles. Leave a little room at the top of the stick to add a flag made from colored tape.

P.S.-
This boat will really float! Make a few and have bathtub races and adventures!

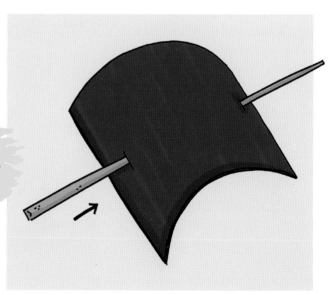

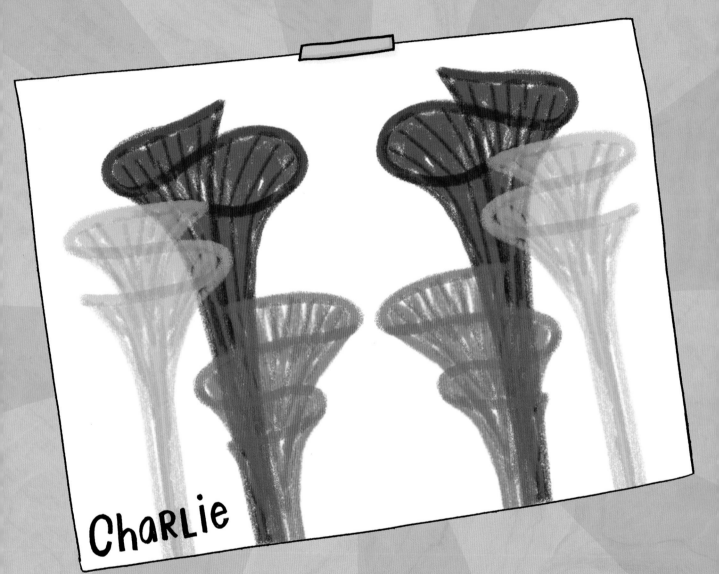

CharLie

ABSTRACT STRING MURALS

It's a blank canvas and you're the artist—no strings attached!

INGREDIENTS

Paper • string • paint • shallow dishes

1. Pour some paint into a shallow dish. Fold your paper in half, then open it up and place it on a flat surface nearby. Dip a piece of cotton string into the paint.

2. Lay the painted string onto the right half your paper in a fun pattern—squiggle it around—leaving some of the string hanging off the bottom of the paper. Fold the paper over and press down on the string evenly.

3. With one hand on top of the paper to steady the string, gently pull the string out from between the paper. Unfold the paper to see the cool string art! Repeat with different pieces of string dipped into other colors and layer to create some out-of-this-world art.

BALLOON SPLATTER ART

Balloons—not just for parties. Fill them with paint and channel your inner Jackson Pollock.

INGREDIENTS

Foam board • tarp • pencil • balloons • funnel • paint • painter's tape

1. Using a funnel, fill balloons about half full with paint, then blow the balloon up the rest of the way. If your paint is too thick, add water to thin it. If you don't have a funnel, cut the bottom off a plastic water bottle, place the balloon around the neck, and use the bottle like a funnel.

2. Knot the balloons and tape them to a piece of foamboard (use the tarp to protect the floor or wall behind the foamboard.) Forcefully pop each with a sharpened pencil and splatter the paint like the true artist you are! Carefully remove the balloons and tape, trying not to disturb your art, when you are finished.

P.S.-
Have an adult help blow up the balloons and be very careful not to inhale or suck in any paint.

MOM, DAD, + LEO Age 3

HAND + FOOTPRINT ANIMALS

**Turn tiny handprints and footprints into lions and tigers and bears, oh my!
Get the whole family in on this one!**

INGREDIENTS

Paper • paper plates • hand wipes • paint • paintbrush • markers

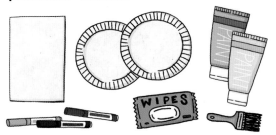

1. Pour a little paint onto a paper plate and spread it around. Place your hands (and, in step 2, your feet) directly in it—you want the paint to spread evenly over your hands/bottom of your feet. (You can also use a paint brush to get the paint to spread evenly.) Cover the paper with colorful handprints and footprints.

2. Repeat with your feet as well—just be sure not to walk on the floor! Use wipes to clean up.

3. When the paint is dry, embellish the hand and footprints to bring them to life as animals by drawing on details using markers. Take it a step farther and frame your family zoo or turn it into wrapping paper!

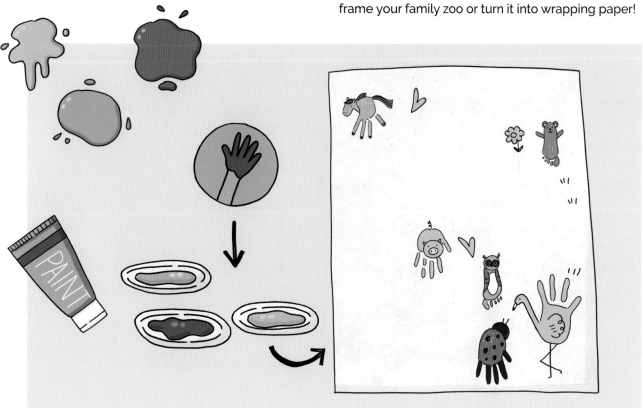

INVISIBLE PAINTING

Keep your masterpiece a secret until the big reveal with the help of white crayons and watercolors.

INGREDIENTS

Paper • white crayon • watercolor paints • paintbrush • water

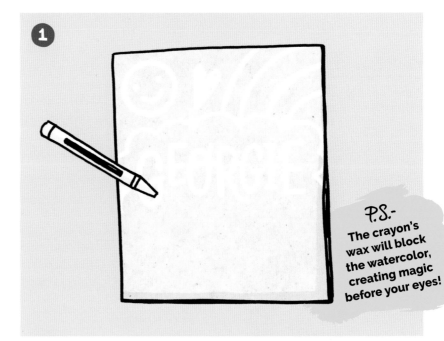

P.S.-
The crayon's wax will block the watercolor, creating magic before your eyes!

1. Using a white crayon, draw a design or message on a piece of paper.

2. Paint all over the paper with watercolor to reveal the invisible design.

TIE-DYE CRAYONS

Bring those broken and old crayons back in action by creating wildly cool shaped crayons with multidimensional mixed hues.

INGREDIENTS

Oven • baking tray • timer • cooking spray • aluminum foil • crayons • cookie cutters

1. Preheat the oven to 350°F (175°C). Coat a baking pan with foil or parchment paper and spread out broken crayon pieces in the pan, making sure to remove any crayon wrappers first. Bake for 10 to 15 minutes, until fully melted.

2. Remove the baking pan from the oven and let cool for about 15 minutes. You don't want the wax to be too soft or too hard. Spray cookie cutters with nonstick spray and press them in the wax to cut out super colorful 3D crayons.

TICK, TOCK!

350

CUT 'EM OUT & LET SET!

MARKER HACKS

On your markers, get set . . . GO! Here are some fun tricks and hacks for any art-loving enthusiast.

HACK

INGREDIENTS

Paper • toilet paper roll tube • painter's tape • markers

Tape markers all the way around a toilet paper roll, making sure to keep the tips all at the same height. This multi-colored and extra-thick marker party is everything!

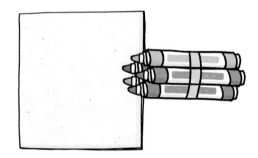

HACK

2

Paper • spray bottle • water • markers

Dried-up markers? Don't throw them away just yet! Place the markers inside a spray bottle (tips down) and add water. The water will be absorbed by the felt in the markers and will hydrate them back to their colorful life, and the ink will tint the water. Spray the tinted water directly onto paper or canvas, or remove the markers from the bottle to color the old-fashioned way again.

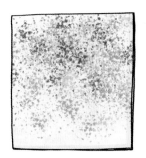

HACK

3

INGREDIENTS

Paper • markers • spray bottle • water • sandwich bag

PRESS

Draw directly onto a sandwich bag with markers. Give the bag a spray of water and press a piece of paper directly onto it for a dreamy watercolor effect!

PAINT HACKS

No paintbrush? No problem! From cotton balls to potato mashers and from carved potatoes to partially cooked pasta, all is fair game when it comes to creativity! Discovering ways to repurpose household items like sponges (and, even, leftover corn on the cob) is not only fun, but a way to explore unique textures and cool effects that a paintbrush simply cannot achieve.

Think of all the other items you have around the house that you could use to paint with—and yes, Mom's closet and jewelry are off-limits.

GET IN THE MOOD TO PLAY WITH FOOD!

Everything tastes better when it's homemade with love, especially pizza, desserts, and fruit when it is in the shape of a BBQ grill! Playing with your food doesn't have to spell trouble if you're learning while being creative. Making your own colors and measuring like a pro might seem like little tasks, but in reality, these activities encourage confidence, help to develop important life skills, and in turn will make kids more excited to enjoy their food when they make it!

P.S.- Do have fun, and don't forget to clean up!

PAINT PALETTE CAKE

Don't wait for a special occasion to celebrate a budding artist in the family.

INGREDIENTS

Cake • plate • icing • icing spatula or knife • butter knife • tiny glass or cookie cutter • food coloring • paintbrush • small cups or dishes

1. Bake a single-layer round cake according to instructions and let it cool completely. Cut the top to make it flat, as shown, then cut a rounded, wavy indent out of one side to create a palette shape and cut out a small hole for the "finger" using a tiny glass or little cookie cutter.

2. Frost the cake completely with white frosting. Divide some of the white frosting among small dishes and mix each one with a different food coloring to create "paint." Add small dollops of colored icing to create paint blotches around the edge of the cake. Display on a cutting board or cake stand with a paintbrush for some extra flair.

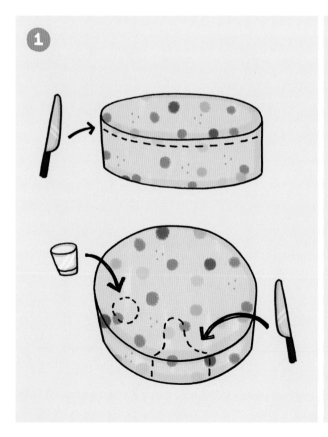

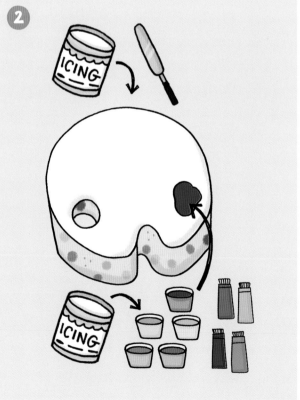

BUTTERFLY CAKE

Any way you slice it, this cake will make hearts flutter.

INGREDIENTS

Cake • **plate** • **butter knife** • **candy stick** • **icing** • **food coloring** • **sprinkles** • **sandwich bag**

1. Bake a single-layer round cake according to instructions and let it cool completely. Cut it in half.

2. Arrange the semicircles on your serving platter with the curved sides touching.

3. Cut each half at an angle and separate the pieces slightly to create top and bottom wings. Cover in frosting and decorate! Add the candy stick between the wings, as shown, to create the butterfly's body.

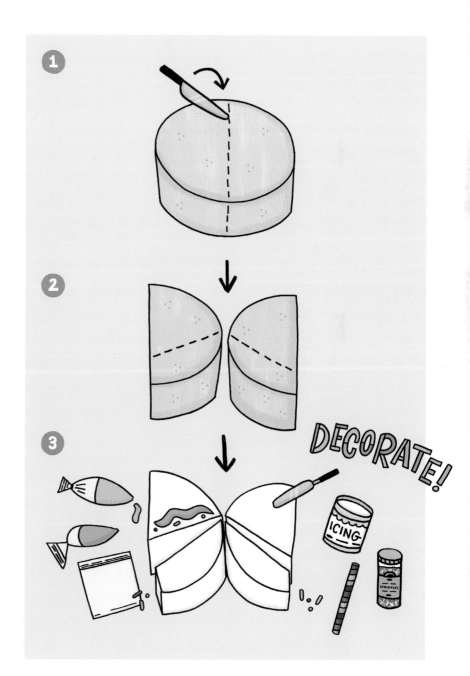

DECORATE!

GARDEN FOCACCIA

Bloom where you're planted . . . or baked!

INGREDIENTS

Oven • **baking tray** • **knife** • **rolling pin** • **pizza dough** • **bell peppers** • **onions** • **olives** • **basil** • **lavender** • **olive oil** • **mozzarella cheese (optional)** •

1. Preheat the oven to 350°F (175°C). Roll out the pizza dough on a greased baking sheet. Drizzle olive oil all over the dough.

2. Cut and arrange your favorite vegetables and toppings to look like flowers and leaves.

3. Bake for 20 minutes or until the crust is lightly browned. Serve a little red sauce on the side for dipping!

P.S.- **Sprinkle cheese in between the vegetables if desired.**

ICE TRAY SUSHI

The coolest way to roll!

INGREDIENTS

Ice cube tray • knife • plastic wrap • rice • sushi-grade salmon and tuna • crab meat • salmon roe • avocado • mango • cucumber • spicy mayo • soy sauce • nori • sesame seeds

1. Line an ice cube tray with a sheet of plastic wrap. Layer in whatever sushi toppings you wish to have in each bite. Next, add a small amount of sushi rice into each section, and cover with a piece of plastic wrap again. Gently press down into each ice cube section to make sure the sushi layers are packed tightly. Refrigerate for 30 minutes to 1 hour to set.

2. Remove the top layer of plastic wrap, then flip the ice cube tray directly onto a platter and slowly remove the sushi pieces from the container by gently removing the plastic wrap. Once each sushi piece has popped out, get to garnishing with spicy mayo, nori, sesame seeds, roe, and your favorite soy and ponzu sauces!

FRUITY BBQ

Now this is what you call a sweet party trick!

INGREDIENTS

Toothpicks • skewers • spoon • knife • watermelon • fruit kabobs • celery • lime • blackberries

1. Slice off the top portion of a watermelon and set aside. Cut three small holes on the bottom of the lower section, equally spaced.

2. Scoop and hollow out both the top and bottom sections. The flesh should be cut into smaller pieces for the kabobs. Insert three equal-sized celery stalks into the holes at the bottom to serve as the legs of the grill. Use toothpicks to help anchor the celery.

3. Fill the bottom section with blackberries (this is the charcoal) and insert wooden skewers on the inside opening to create the "grill." Create the grill's handle by affixing a lime wedge to the top using toothpicks.

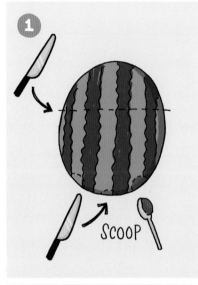

1

SCOOP

2

SCOOP

3

4

P.S.-
You will have to cut or break the skewers into smaller pieces toward the sides.

4. Place the fruit kabobs directly on the grill. Break a skewer in half and use it to prop up the lid of the BBQ by inserting the two pieces underneath the hollow top and pushing them into the bases rind. Everyone will be fired up for this treat!

VEGGIE TRAIN

Ain't no party like a veggie party! Be the host with the most creative hors d'oeuvres display.

INGREDIENTS

Knife • spoon • toothpicks • ranch dressing • watermelon • strawberries • blueberries • bananas • radish • bell peppers • broccoli • cucumbers • celery • carrots • snow peas • carrots • cherry tomatoes • cilantro

1. Using a knife and spoon, cut and hollow out cucumbers, peppers, and/or watermelon for trains. Use toothpicks to attach "wheels."

2. Get creative with what items you already have in your kitchen to make these choo-choos come to life! Arrange on a large cutting board for serving.

SCOOP!

RAINBOW WAFFLES

Brighten up any morning with a little ROYGBIV and extra whipped cream.

INGREDIENTS

Waffle maker · knife · scissors · mixing bowl · small bowls · waffle batter · food coloring · sandwich bags · whipped cream · sprinkles

1. Divide your favorite waffle batter among several small bowls. Add 1 to 3 drops of food coloring to each and mix to create the colors of the rainbow. Pour each color of batter into its own sandwich bag.

2. Preheat the waffle iron. Pour red batter around the outside edge of the waffle iron, followed by a ring of orange, then yellow, and continue to make rings around in rainbow color order. The final color to add should be purple at the center.

3. Close the waffle iron and cook according to the manufacturer's directions. When done, remove it from the waffle iron and slice the waffle in half to create two rainbows. Add whipped cream and sprinkles to the bottom half of each waffle to make dreamy (and delicious) clouds. Repeat with remaining batter.

COOK!

P.S.-
If you have a very steady hand, you can skip the piping bags and use a spoon.

KITTY BREAD BOWL

A snack that's the cat's meow!

INGREDIENTS

Loaf of bread • bowl • knife • toothpicks • chocolate chips • carrots • celery • candy • veggie dip

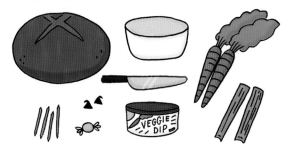

1. Cut the top off a round loaf of bread. Do not throw away the top—that will be your kitty's head.

2. Use a knife to cut and hollow out the bottom of the loaf to make a bowl. Use some of the bread's insides to cut out triangle kitty ears and a cute tail. Dice the rest of the bread to serve alongside, for dipping.

3. Create a face with chocolate chips for the eyes and a candy nose—use a dab of veggie dip to get them to stick to the bread. Whiskers could be toothpicks, or add some color and use chives. Fill the bowl with your favorite dip, place it inside the hollowed out loaf, and enjoy with the bread cubes and cut veggies!

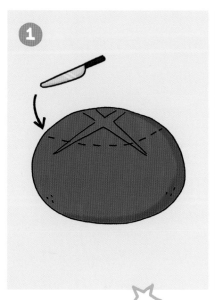

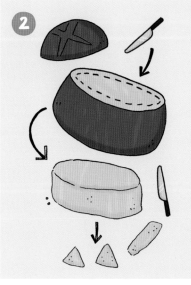

FILL WITH DIP!

BAGEL BUDDIES

Whoever told you not to play with your food was 100 percent wrong.

FROGGY BAGEL

INGREDIENTS

Bagels • bowl • knife • cream cheese • chives • olives • bell pepper • cucumber

Chop the chives and mix them into cream cheese then spread it on a bagel. Cut a cucumber in half. Cut one half into rounds for eyes. Cut the other half lengthwise to create legs. Make a smile out of piece of a pepper and finish off with sliced olives for eyes.

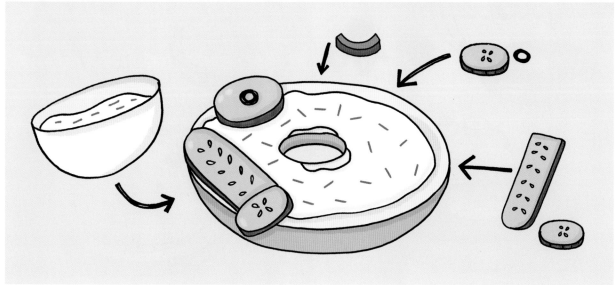

OWL BAGEL

INGREDIENTS

Bagels • knife • spoon • peanut butter • banana • strawberries • blueberries

Spread peanut butter on a bagel. Top banana slices with blueberries for eyes; cut a strawberry in half for a beak; slice two more strawberry pieces for wings.

PIGGY BAGEL

INGREDIENTS

Bagels • knife • lunchmeat • cheese • olives • radish • chives

Spread a light layer of butter or mayonnaise on a bagel (optional). Top with a round of ham or your favorite lunchmeat for the face, cut a piece of cheese into a snout, halve olives for the eyes, cut pieces of lunchmeat for the ears, and add a small piece of radish for the inner ear. Don't forget to curl a chive around your finger to make a curly tail.

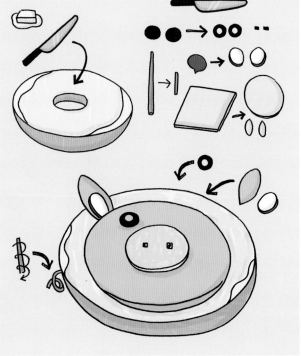

DESSERT TREAT BOWLS

A twist on a classic treat that's sure to bowl you over.

INGREDIENTS

Crispy rice cereal · butter · marshmallows · chocoloate melts · plastic wrap · two bowls · spoon

1. Line a large bowl with plastic wrap.

2. In a separate large bowl, melt 3 tablespoons butter and 4 cups (200 g) mini marshmallows together using the microwave. Mix in 6 cups (180 g) crispy rice cereal.

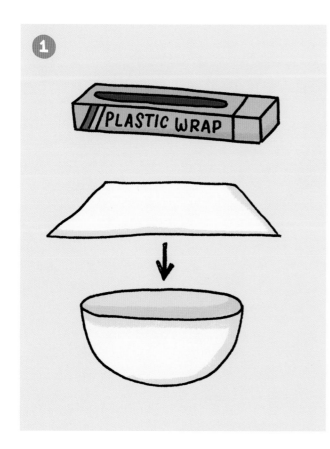

3. Add the crispy rice mixture to the plastic-lined bowl while it's still warm and press it into the sides and bottom to make a bowl shape. A smaller bowl pressed into the larger bowl will make quick work of this.

4. In a separate small bowl, melt about 1 cup of chocolate in the microwave to a liquid consistency and coat the inside of the crispy rice bowl using the back of a spoon. Refrigerate the chocolate for 30 minutes to harden fully, then fill with a delicious treat such as ice cream, pudding, or even chocolate-covered strawberries.

MOLD!

CHOCOLATE MELTS

COAT INSIDE

P.S.-
Put bowls in the fridge to harden before placing dessert inside.

FOSSIL SUGAR COOKIES

Nothing to see here folks, just some sweet prehistoric nibbles.

INGREDIENTS

Oven • **sugar cookie batter** • **baking sheet** • **parchment paper** • **cookie scoop** • **toy animal figures**

1. Bake your favorite sugar cookie recipe according to instructions—anything works!

2. Once removed from the oven but while still warm, press a small plastic bug, insect, or mini dinosaur toy directly into the cookie then remove it. This will leave an imprint, creating edible fossils for you to observe and gobble up.

PIZZA TREATS

In pizza we crust.

INGREDIENTS

Crispy rice treat base or vanilla cake • icing • red food coloring • black licorice • green sour straws • red licorice wheels • coconut flakes

1. Choose a vanilla cake or crispy rice treat base for your "pie crust." Whichever you use, be sure to have it in a circular baking pan. Create a deep-dish style indent by carving out some of the inside, leaving a crust edge.

2. Mix red food coloring into white frosting for pizza sauce and spread it on the crust.

3. Sprinkle coconut flakes on top of the "sauce" for cheese.

4. Top off with pieces of candy such as red licorice wheels (pepperoni), sliced sour straws (green peppers), and black licorice sticks cut into rings (olives).

SPAGHETTI BOWLS

The filling *pastabilities* are truly endless . . .

INGREDIENTS

Oven • spaghetti • salt • bowls • wooden spoon • measuring cups • cheese • egg

1. Preheat the oven to 350°F (175°C). Cook the spaghetti in a large pot of boiling water salted according to the directions on the box.

2. Mix ½ cup (50 g) grated parmesan cheese, 1½ cups (165 g) shredded mozzarella, and 1 egg together in an oven-safe bowl. Add the cooked pasta and mix together thoroughly.

3. Place a smaller bowl into the pasta mixture and press so the pasta takes the shape of the bowl. Remove the inner bowl when the shape is formed. Bake for 20 minutes. Remove from the oven and enjoy with your favorite pasta toppings.

MIX!

TICK, TOCK!

UNICORN LEMONADE

Magical hues of purple, pink, and blue, all created and enjoyed by you!

INGREDIENTS

Pitchers • measuring cup • tea strainer • filtered water • sugar • lemons • dried butterfly pea flowers

1. Bring 3 cups (720 ml) water and 1 cup (200 g) sugar to a boil. Stir in about ½ cup (40 g) dried butterfly pea flowers and boil until a dark blue color appears. Remove from the heat, cover, and let steep for approximately 10 minutes. Strain the tea, discarding all of the flower pieces, and let cool.

2. Combine 1 cup (240 ml) lemon juice with 2 cups (480 ml) filtered water.

3. To create magical lemonade, pour butterfly pea flower syrup over ice in a glass, filling the glass halfway.

4. Add lemon water to fill the glass to the top and watch the blue turn to purple before your eyes!

P.S.-
How does this magic work!? Pea flowers have a special plant pigment called anthocyanin. When the pH of the blue tea is changed by the lemon juice, it transforms into a vibrant magenta.

YUM! YUM! GIMME SOME! 173

WATERCOLOR CAKE

Totally to dye for!

INGREDIENTS

Vanilla cake or brownies • white icing • icing spatula or knife • food coloring

OR

1. Frost a cake with white frosting (or buy one!). Sprinkle drops of food coloring over it. (Frosted brownies work, too!)

2. With an icing spatula or flat knife, make long strokes across the cake to create a watercolor effect. The more you spread, the more the colors will bleed together.

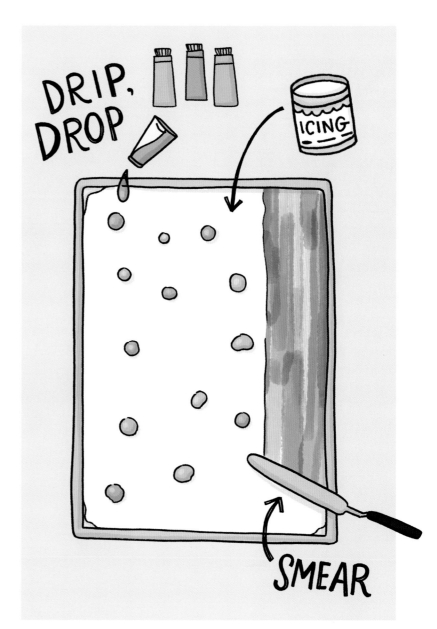

DRIP, DROP

ICING

SMEAR

ALPHABET FRUIT KABOBS

What did the watermelon say to the pineapple? *Spell ya later.*

INGREDIENTS

Watermelon · cantaloupe · pineapple · mango · blueberries · raspberries · cookie cutter letters · skewers

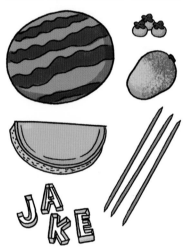

1. Cut fruit slices (watermelon, cantaloupe, pineapple) approximately 1 to 2 inches (2.5 to 5 cm) thick. Use alphabet cookie cutters to punch out letters.

2. Spell out names and words with the fruit letters directly onto wooden skewers. Add blueberries or raspberries to complete the skewers. Fill glasses with ice and your favorite beverage and add a fruit skewer to each.

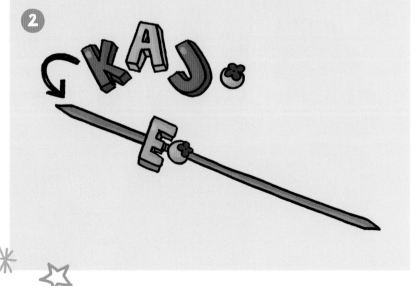

VEGGIE GARDEN SNACK

Bringing a whole new meaning to "farm to table."

INGREDIENTS

Terra-cotta pot • coffee filter or wax paper • blender • bread • asparagus • radishes • carrots • dip

1. Line a terra-cotta pot with a coffee filter or wax paper.

2. Blend dark-colored bread slices (pumpernickel is ideal) in a blender to make bread crumb "soil."

3. "Plant" fresh vegetables directly into the "soil" and pair with a yummy dip on the side.

FISHBOWL CAKE

Nothing fishy about this dessert—it's *oh-fish-al*, anyone can decorate a cake!

INGREDIENTS

Round cake • butter knife • icing knife • fruit rolls • candy straws • icing • food coloring • sandwich bags • scissors

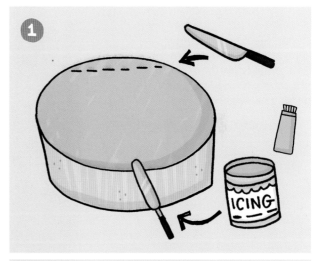

1. Cut off the top of a round cake to create a fishbowl shape. Frost the entire cake with light blue frosting.

2. Bring the cake to life by adding details and textures using candy and icing—fish out of fruit rolls and candy eyes, water ripples with darker hues of blue icing (use sandwich bags as piping bags), seaweed made from twisted sour straws.

SPORTY HAND PIES

If it involves pie dough, I'm pretty sure it's a home run.

INGREDIENTS

Oven • pie dough • icing • icing spatula or knife • spoon • fork • cookie cutter or drinking glass • pie filling • egg wash • brush • piping bag

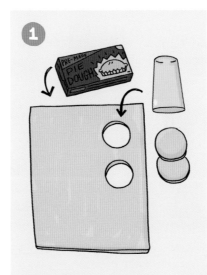

1. Preheat the oven to 350°F (175°C). Unroll pre-made, room-temperature pie dough and cut out circles using a circular cookie cutter or the top of a drinking glass. You will need two circles for each pie.

SEAL

2. Add your favorite pie filling or fresh fruit sprinkled with brown sugar to the center of one circle. Cover the top with the second pie circle, and pinch the edges together with your fingers or a fork.

BRUSH ON EGG WASH BAKE!

COOL & DECORATE!

3. Brush the top and sides with an egg wash, then prick the top with a fork to let steam out. Bake for 30 minutes.

4. Let the pies cool completely before decorating with icing to look like the ball from your favorite sport.

P.S.-
Make your own royal icing!
1½ cups (180 g) powdered sugar
2 tablespoons (30 ml) warm water
½ tablespoon (10 g) light corn syrup
⅛ teaspoon vanilla extract

Use a mixer to blend everything until smooth.

HAPPY CRAFTERNOON!

BACK TO THE BASICS

Did you spill your jar of bubbles? We got you.

Are you fresh out of glue or hand sanitizer and don't feel like to running to the store? No sweat.

Do your kids need to mix, smush, paint, play, and create and you're fresh out of simple ideas? We got you.

Here's some basic craft-math that will help you out in a pinch. Chances are, you probably have all of these ingredients on hand already.

BUBBLE LIQUID

INGREDIENTS

3 cups (720 ml) warm water
½ cup (120 ml) corn syrup
½ cup (120 ml) dish soap

In a reusable container, combine the water, corn syrup, and dish soap.

GLUE

INGREDIENTS

¾ cup (180 ml) water
2 tablespoons corn syrup
1 teaspoon white vinegar
½ cup (65 g) cornstarch mixed with ¾ cup (180 ml) cold water

In a bowl, combine the water, corn syrup, vinegar, and the cornstarch mixture; stir until smooth.

HAND SANITIZER

INGREDIENTS

⅔ cup (165 ml) rubbing alcohol
⅓ cup (75 ml) aloe vera
10 drops essential oil of choice

In a reusable container, combine the rubbing alcohol, aloe vera, and essential oil. If you want it to be more liquid, add more rubbing alcohol. If you prefer a gel, add more aloe.

FAKE SNOW

INGREDIENTS

3 cups (540 g) baking soda
½ cup (120 ml) hair conditioner
OR
1 part shaving cream
1 part cornstarch

In a bowl, combine the ingredients
a little at a time, mixing slowly,
until the mixture looks like snow.

SLIME

INGREDIENTS

1 cup (240 ml) clear glue
1 tablespoon baking soda
Contact solution, or 1 tablespoon
salt mixed with 1 tablespoon water
until the salt is dissolved to make
a saline solution
Food coloring

In a bowl, combine the glue
and baking soda until smooth.
Add the contact solution to
activate the slime.

PUFFY SLIME

INGREDIENTS

⅔ cup (165 ml) glue
½ teaspoon baking soda
¼ cup (60 ml) water
2 cups (480 ml) shaving cream
1½ tablespoons contact solution
Food coloring

In a bowl, combine the glue, baking
soda, water, and shaving cream
until smooth. Add the contact
solution to activate
the slime.

PLAY DOUGH

INGREDIENTS

2 cups (250 g) flour

¾ cup (165 g) salt

4 teaspoons cream of tartar

2 cups (480 ml) lukewarm water

2 tablespoons vegetable or coconut oil

Sandwich bags

Food coloring

In a large pot, combine the flour, salt, cream of tartar, water, and oil. Cook over medium heat, stirring constantly, until the dough has thickened, about 30 seconds to 2 minutes. Remove from the heat. When cool enough to handle, knead the dough until smooth. Separate into individual sandwich bags and add food coloring to each bag, kneading it into a dough to make fun colors.

PUFFY PAINT

INGREDIENTS

¾ cup (180 ml) shaving cream

¼ cup (60 ml) white glue

¼ cup (30 g) flour

Food coloring

In a large bowl, combine the shaving cream, glue, and flour. Divide among small bowls (or use a muffin tin), adding food coloring to each bowl to create fun colors. If you want to go the extra mile, transfer to squeeze bottles instead of bowls.

SALT DOUGH
(HANDPRINTS + ORNAMENTS)

Preheat the oven to 200°F (95°C). In a large bowl, combine the flour, salt, and water. Knead with your hands for at least 10 minutes to form a dough. Transfer it to a lightly floured surface, roll it out ¼ inch (6 mm) thick, cut out with cookie cutters, and bake for 1 to 2 hours (see note). Let cool completely, then use acrylic paint to decorate.

NOTE: Baking times can range from 1 to 2 hours depending on thickness of dough and the oven. Check after 1 hour to see if hardened. If not, continue to bake until hard.

INGREDIENTS

4 cups (500 g) flour

1 cup (220 g) salt

1½ cups (360 ml) water

Acrylic paint

P.S.-
Seal the finished product with Mod Podge so these will last for years.

AIR DRY CLAY

INGREDIENTS

2 cups (360 g) baking soda

1 cup (130 g) cornstarch, plus more for dusting your work surface

1½ cups (360 ml) water

In a pot over medium heat, combine the baking soda, cornstarch, and water, stirring until the mixture is smooth and a dough ball forms, about 10 minutes. Remove from the heat when it becomes sticky and soft. You may need to keep stirring or knead until no longer tacky. Transfer the dough to a cornstarch-coated surface and mold it into your desired shapes. Let your pieces sit out for 2 to 3 days, until fully dry.

PAPIER-MÂCHÉ PASTE

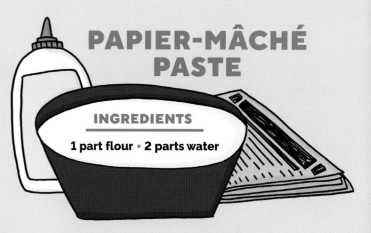

INGREDIENTS

1 part flour • 2 parts water

In a large bowl, whisk together the flour and water, making sure to get out all the lumps. The consistency should be thin, like pancake batter.

P.S.-
If the glue smell is bothersome, add a dash of cinnamon or a drop of vanilla extract.

SIDEWALK CHALK PAINT

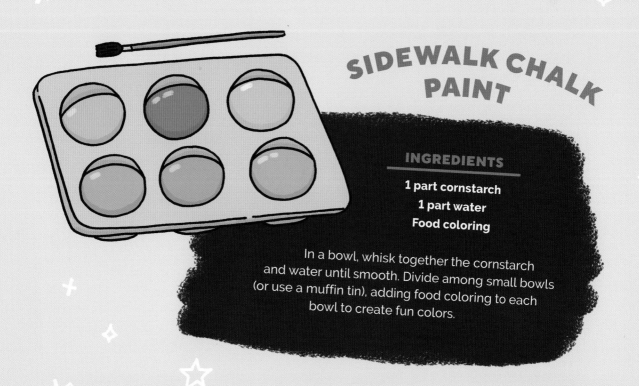

INGREDIENTS

1 part cornstarch

1 part water

Food coloring

In a bowl, whisk together the cornstarch and water until smooth. Divide among small bowls (or use a muffin tin), adding food coloring to each bowl to create fun colors.

ABOUT THE AUTHOR

ERICA DOMESEK is Wylie's mom and the founder of the innovative do-it-yourself (DIY) lifestyle brand P.S.- I Made This, which launched in 2009. P.S.- I Made This was born from Erica's passion for hand-making beautiful accessories, décor, cooking, and entertaining that make everyday life more colorful and fun. She has been a distinguished expert in the areas of design and style as well as a leader in brand marketing for fifteen years. Her personal mission is to inspire and encourage people everywhere to embrace the concept of *crafting the life they want*. She has helped develop and execute hundreds of successful digital and experiential programs with top-tier brands looking to align themselves with connected and passionate audiences. Domesek has appeared on the *Today* show, *Rachael Ray*, *The Martha Stewart Show*, *E! News*, and more! Her work has been featured in issues of *Vogue*, *Glamour*, *Domino*, the *Wall Street Journal*, *Self*, *Elle*, *Teen Vogue*, and more. She has published two best-selling books, but her favorite project of all . . . is Wylie!

ACKNOWLEDGMENTS

P.S.- I ^(couldn't have) made this ... without you!

The juggle is real! Navigating everyday life during a global pandemic while trying to work, parent, and show up for family and friends while working on this book was nothing short of a personal typhoon. Some days it felt like I was blindly navigating the open seas on a raft made of sticks and string (P.S.- **I have made one of those before**). I am immensely grateful for those who helped me in some way to bring this project to life and stay on course. These people were the glue to my cracks, and the brackets who helped me keep it together both literally and physically.

Thank you to Steph Stilwell, my illustrator and collaborator extraordinaire. You brought this vision to life and so much more! Your genuine love for quirky art and willingness to dive right into things is what sets you apart from everyone. Dream team!

Thank you to Shawna, my editor, who got a master's in patience while working on this project. Thank you for your endless support on this book.

Mom, I'm sorry for drawing on the walls with Sharpies and crayons when I was little. Most importantly, thank you for always encouraging me to live in color!

Michael, thank you for always being there to spell-check, support me, do the dishes, and be my #1 champion for this book and everything else. P.S.- **You still can't draw a bench . . .**

Thank you to Ariel, for pushing me to be the best version of myself. For holding my hand, having my back, and forever being there for palomas and hugs. ILYSM.

A million thank-yous to you, Dr. Laurel Felt. Collaborating on this was incredibly special. May our shared love for helping kids thrive, create, learn, and inspire play never end!

P.S.- **Special acknowledgments:** My loving and supportive family, Anthony Mattero, Boo Simms, Tania Sinzu, Niki Sepanj, Nan Khanna, Hailey Turpin, Jenny Meyer Czarny, Samantha Berger, MAJE, ELDISCOTECA, and last but not least, my UPS man Zoltan, who delivers so many packages and boxes to my door that get repurposed into amazing things!

XO

@psimadethis

P.S.- Can't wait to see your creations!
#pswemadethis